TEACHER'S BOOK

Brainwaves

LEVEL 3

OXFORD UNIVERSITY PRESS 1998

Hancock & Miller ••••••• Wakeman & Kozanoglou

Teacher's Book Contents

Contents

unit	Vocabulary *topic*	*lexical area*	Language focus	Skills focus
11	**Dear Sue ...** • describing personality and mood	• connotation *(positive and negative)*	**A radio phone-in** • *If I were you ...* making suggestions and giving advice	**Odd one out** • reading for information • letter writing • discussion
12	**Can you believe it?** • expressing belief and disbelief • achievements	• pronunciation *(expressing meaning through stress and intonation)*	**Golden boy Marcus** • present perfect (experiences and achievements)	**Truth or fiction?** • listening for key words • writing, speaking and listening
13	**The secrets of your dreams** • dream images • reactions to dreams	• word grammar *(-ing forms: verbal nouns)*	**Dream on** • present perfect and past simple	**A book of dreams** • reading for information • song: *Octopus's Garden* • project: a book of dreams
14	**The body beautiful** • fitness activities	• register *(colloquial expressions)*	**Harry and Bill** • *used to*	**An interview with Will Murphy** • predicting and reading • pronunciation (*stress: information-carrying words*) • role-play • song: *Walking on Sunshine*
15	**Coping with exams** • exam techniques	• collocation • paraphrasing • phrases with *get*	**Five steps to relieving exam stress** • 2nd conditional	**Improve your revision techniques** • predicting and listening • reading and speaking • writing a magazine article

PROJECTS
- Films
- Game Shows
- Food
- Magazines

GRAMMAR SUMMARY

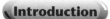

Introduction

Brainwaves is a three-level English language course designed for young learners. The three levels are:

Brainwaves 1   – for beginners
Brainwaves 2   – for elementary students
Brainwaves 3   – for pre-intermediate students.

At each level, the course consists of the following components:

- Student's Book
- Cassettes
- Workbook
- Teacher's Book.

Language focus of *Brainwaves 3*

Brainwaves 3 is the pre-intermediate level of an English language course designed for young students. It is intended to provide approximately 100 hours of classroom instruction, but this time can (and should) be adapted to suit your own particular teaching situation and syllabus requirements.

Listening skills are developed by specific tasks associated with the material recorded on the cassette.

Speaking activities are given great importance throughout the course, with many activities involving pair or group work as well as whole class feedback and discussion.

Writing tasks are initially quite simple (for example, requiring students to supply personal information, make short notes and complete short gap-fill exercises), but quickly develop in complexity to include summaries, project work and paragraphs of description, narrative and dialogue.

Reading skills are practised in every unit, with texts gradually becoming longer and more complex in structure. There is a variety of text types, including forms, questionnaires and letters, as well as descriptive passages and stories.

Students are also introduced to a number of **learning skills/strategies**. The units suggest useful listening and reading tips and provide guidance in note-taking, organizational skills (e.g. ways of categorizing vocabulary) and co-operative skills (e.g. through pair and group work).

Brainwaves 3 course components

Student's Book

There are 15 main units in Brainwaves 3 and each of these, is organized in three sections:

- **Vocabulary:** this section introduces the general theme of the unit and familiarizes students with new lexis. It also deals with particular lexical areas such as colocation or word attack skills.
- **Language focus:** this section provides a graded presentation of new structures and functions.
- **Skills focus:** this section gives students the opportunity to see and practise the new language in context, with a range of tasks that engage all four skills.

Other features are as follows:

- 'Focus' boxes, where general language rules are set out, with examples
- 'Look!' boxes, which spotlight certain features of the new language, usually through examples
- 'Think about it!' boxes, which summarize the main language point of the unit and encourage students to check and evaluate their progress.

There is no continuous storyline in Brainwaves 3, but the character Sparks, introduced in Brainwaves 1, appears at regular intervals in the course of the book to illustrate the concept behind the new structures. While the units are organized sequentially around particular language areas, they also each develop a certain theme.

Regular Revision units appear after Units 5, 10 and 15.

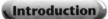

Cassettes

There are two cassettes which contain all listening texts, pronunciation tasks, songs and chants for this level. An icon in the Student's Book identifies the material that is recorded on the cassette.

Workbook

The Workbook provides additional reading and writing practice in the language items presented in the Student's Book through a variety of tasks. Two special features of the Workbook (named after *Brainwaves* characters) are:

- 'Buzz words', a puzzle which focuses on the vocabulary of the unit
- 'Flick back!' which encourages the students to check their answers to the Workbook tasks.

Teacher's Book

This Teacher's Book contains:

- complete teaching notes with suggestions for using the Student's Book and Workbook materials
- photocopiable tests
- extra photocopiable activities for classroom use
- an alphabetical word list with unit references to indicate where the words first appear.

The teaching notes for each unit consist of the following:

- Learning objectives – these outline the functional aims of each unit.
- Language focus – this lists the main areas of grammar and word grammar focused on in the unit.
- Active vocabulary – an alphabetical list of the vocabulary items that students are expected to learn and use actively in speaking and writing. This list can also be used as a checklist of lexical items for testing purposes.
- Receptive vocabulary – these vocabulary items are intended for recognition only. Many of the items are included in written rubrics, and need not be tested.
- Materials – a checklist of the materials needed for the suggested activities in the teaching notes.
- Lead-ins – these are different options for introducing the students to the new unit.
- Background information – where appropriate, this section gives extra information about areas such as cultural features, style and register of language items, or concepts and objects that may be unfamiliar to the students.
- Tapescripts – these give the complete written version of all the materials on tape.

- Notes – where appropriate, these notes highlight features such as potential learner difficulties and suggested solutions, useful hints concerning the teaching of the language items and reminders to ask students to bring in materials for the next lesson.
- Answers – here you will find all the suggested answers to the tasks in the Student's Book.
- Workbook answers – suggested answers to tasks in the Workbook.
- Additional activities – these are designed to provide either extra material or alternative materials for practice, allowing you to adapt the course to suit your class and timetable.

Main units: suggested teaching procedures

Lead-ins

In order to establish a contextual and linguistic basis for each new unit, begin with a lead-in activity: this might be revision of previously-taught language which is relevant to the lesson, or an activity which anticipates the focus of the new unit. A number of options are suggested in the teaching notes. You don't have to teach all of them: just choose one, or combine ideas to design your own lead-in activity.

Using the cassette

First listening

When using the cassette, always give the students a task before they listen. This not only provides them with a reason for listening, but enables them to focus on the most important parts of the tapescript without worrying about every detail. For example, they can describe the picture, and if appropriate, speculate what the people might be saying. Or you could set a simple question for them to answer.

Second listening

Whereas the first listening focuses students on the content of the tapescript, the second listening allows them to think about details of the more specific language items. Before asking them to listen again, set specific questions, for example, *What does she/he say (about . . .)?*

Reading dialogue

Where the tapescripts contain dialogue, encourage students to take roles and read the words aloud, using the cassette as a model for pronunciation. This reading of the dialogue enables them to make associations between the sounds and the written script, and also allows them to 'have a go' at producing the new language without being concerned about form and grammar.

Some possible techniques for dialogue reading are as follows:

- Choral/individual repetition – play a line of the dialogue on the cassette, pause the recorder, ask students to repeat all together first, then invite individuals to repeat.

- Group reading – in small groups, with books open, students take a role each and read the dialogue. An alternative is for students to have books closed except for one person in each group who is appointed as prompter and has the book open. The others take a role each and try to remember the lines of the dialogue. If they forget their lines, the prompter can tell them what to say.

- If students are unsure about how to say the lines, try 'ghost-reading' first. Play the cassette, and ask students to mouth the words only. Do this a couple of times, until they feel more confident. Then go on to choral or individual repetition, or group reading.

- Encourage the students to mime the actions, gestures and facial expressions to accompany the dialogue. They can do this while listening to the cassette, or while listening to a group reading aloud. Finally, get them to act out the dialogue, saying the lines and doing the actions.

Teaching vocabulary

When teaching vocabulary, try to make the presentation of the new word as vivid and memorable as possible, for example, by using pictures (either from the Student's Book or from sources of your own), by using mime, or by contextualizing the word in an interesting and familiar anecdote or situation.

Always check that students understand the word or phrase. This can be done in a number of ways, for example:

- With lexical sets/word families that have been presented through pictures, jumble the order of the pictures and ask students at random for the words.

- Give the word and ask students to point to the correct picture.

- Use mime to elicit the word/phrase or give the word/phrase and ask students to mime it.

- Ask students for the word in their L1.

- Ask students to make up a sentence which clearly illustrates the meaning/use of the item.

- Ask students for an example of the item. For example, when teaching *volcano*, ask them for the name of a famous volcano.

- Ask simple concept questions to ensure they have understood the meaning. For example, when teaching *phobia*, ask: *What is a common phobia? What is the difference between a fear and a phobia?*

If the item is for active use, make sure that the students have an opportunity to use it in a practice task during the lesson.

Negotiable vocabulary

Encourage students to ask for new words they need that aren't in the Student's Book. This 'negotiable' element allows them to learn vocabulary of their own choice and for their own needs. Provide words they request, and encourage them to write the words down. These words do not necessarily have to be learnt by all the class, and are not intended for testing purposes.

Pronunciation

When focusing on pronunciation, always check that students can hear and distinguish the sounds. Pronunciation problems are often due to the fact that a sound in English does not exist in the students' mother tongue, or an intonation pattern is different and the students are not aware of this. Once they can actually hear the sound/pattern, encourage them to repeat it in isolation before asking them to incorporate it into a word or phrase.

Songs

Songs provide an enjoyable way of practising or learning new language. The songs in the book are usually accompanied by tasks which help the students to understand the overall meaning. It is not necessary for them to understand every word of the song: play it a few times and encourage them to join in as much as they can. They will gradually pick up the words, and they can hum or sing 'la-la' to the parts they don't yet know. You can ask groups of students to sing different lines, to help them become more familiar with the lyrics.

Look!

The 'Look!' boxes highlight features of the language in focus. When students read these boxes, set them a question to answer beforehand, to direct them to notice the feature and get them thinking. Check their understanding with concept questions.

Think about it!

This regular feature appears at the end of every unit, and provides an opportunity for the students to:

- think about and reflect on what they have done in the unit

- check that they have understood and can use the target language of the unit

- refer back to and revise sections of the unit if they are having difficulty

- evaluate how easy or difficult they found the language and the tasks
- evaluate their own progress.

The tasks are not intended to be tests – students can refer back to previous sections if they need to. If they want to test themselves, they can, but they should not be obliged to do this.

The three pictures of Watt indicate how easy or difficult the unit was – students choose and circle the one that most closely reflects their personal evaluation.

Additional activities

Extra or alternative materials are provided by way of the 'Additional activities' in the Teacher's Book. Some of these are pairwork activities using the Photocopiable Pages at the back of the book.

You can use these materials in class to provide extra practice, or to replace activities in the Student's Book if you prefer. (Further ideas for adapting materials for your class can be found in 'Other useful ideas and techniques' below.)

Revision units: suggested teaching procedures

Revision units appear after every five units, and recycle and consolidate the language from previous units.

At the beginning of each Revision unit, the 'Stop and think!' section provides a 'Help' menu to encourage the students to reflect on what they have done and what they still need to do. After Unit 5, invite the students to quickly look through the Revision unit and show them what it contains. Explain how they will use the 'Stop and think!' section:

1 They work through the practice tasks (in class or at home) and check the answers with you, then work out the number of right answers.

2 If they have got all the answers right, they follow the 'OK' line from the relevant section title to the box with the letter and colour it in. If they have got some answers wrong, they should follow the 'Help' line to the corresponding menu, read the advice and do what it says.

3 When students have coloured in all the letters, they can feel satisfied that they are ready to continue to the next unit.

Other useful ideas and techniques

Adapting the Student's Book material for your class

No coursebook can ever be perfect for every class of learners, so it makes sense to think about the material in advance and make adjustments to it if you feel it is necessary. The material should be viewed as a basis for

your lesson and we hope that your students will find it enjoyable, but we would also hope that you will feel free to adapt the material to make it as suitable as possible for your students. Here are a few ideas for adaptation. Some of the ideas involve the use of a photocopier.

Homework ideas

Exercises from the Workbook can be set as homework, as well as tasks in 'Think about it!' sections in the Student's Book. You can also devise extra written tasks based on the unit topic and material, such as situational dialogues or pictures and descriptions.

Always check that the students are sure about what to do for homework: explain the task, and demonstrate how to do one or two items at least. You may wish to go through the exercises orally in class and have the students write the answers at home.

Dictation techniques

The most common way of giving dictation is for the teacher to read the text aloud and the students to write it down. This is best done as a three-phase activity.

1 Read the text once at normal speed. Students listen only.

2 Read the text in 'chunks' or units of meaning, using commas and full stops as a guide. Students write the phrases as they hear them.

3 Read the text once more at normal speed. Students correct their work, or fill in parts they missed first time.

If dictation is a regular part of your teaching or testing routine, try ringing the changes with these suggestions:

- Use pictures, either small pictures cut out from magazines or your own drawings or illustrations chosen from the book. Give one picture to each student, who should not let anyone else see it. In pairs, students take turns to describe the picture using previously-taught language, and to listen and write the sentences. At the end, they check each other's work, looking for corrections to errors and using their pictures as support for meaning.

- Speed dictation: read a short text once or twice at normal speed. Students write down any words they can and leave spaces for the parts they missed. Pairs compare their notes and add anything their partner has. Papers can be compared with other students' and words added. Read the text once more, and have students try to complete the text as far as possible.

- Instead of taking all the papers in for correction, give out a correct version of the text and ask students in pairs to compare their versions and correct them.

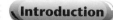

Class revision techniques

Vocabulary revision

- Adapt material from the Student's Book. Photocopy the pictures and blank out the words, then ask students to remember and write the words. As an easier alternative, provide the words in jumbled order.

- Play a guessing game. Demonstrate first, then let students take over. Say, for example, *My word begins with S!* Students then try to guess the word. When they have found it, ask them to use the word in a sentence or phrase.

- Students draw a picture of an object or mime an action, and ask others for the word.

- Have students make cards with words on one side and meanings (in English words or example sentences, in pictures or in L1 translation) on the other. The cards can be used for pair or group games. A student shows one side of the card, and others say what is on the back. Or the cards can be placed on a table, and students take turns to pick one up and say what is on the other side. Another version is to put cards on the table and have students study them for one minute. Then one person takes some out or moves them around while the other students look away. The others then look again and say what has changed or what is missing.

- Devise (or ask the students to devise) picture crosswords or word squares using recently-taught vocabulary, and give them to others to work out.

- Students can make up their own quizzes: they can either provide the meaning (in L1 or English) and ask others for the word, or give a sentence with a blank (indicated by a pause) while others give the missing word.

Revision of other material

- As for vocabulary, oral blank-fills can be devised to practise grammar as well.

- Miming games can also be used for structures.

- Noughts and crosses can be adapted to revise a number of language items. Draw two 3 x 3 grids on the board, and fill one grid with items for revision, for example, a series of simple pictures to be identified or words to be used in sentences. Teams (0s and Xs) take turns to choose a square from the completed grid, and supply the word or a correct sentence using the word. If this answer is correct, fill the corresponding square in the other grid with an 0 or an X. The first team to get a straight line of Xs or 0s is the winner.

Organizing students' notebooks

Suggest that students have different notebooks for classwork, homework and vocabulary. Encourage them to write the date each time they use them, and write a reference to the relevant unit/page of the Student's Book or Workbook. Ask them to use different coloured pens or pencils to highlight headings and features of language they should remember. Make sure that students all have homework tasks written down correctly, and know when to give the work in before they leave the lesson.

For vocabulary, get them to organize the vocabulary notebook into sections, for example, a section for words organized according to the unit/page in the book; another section for words organized according to topic; another for word grammar (e.g. prepositions, pronouns) or for everyday expressions.

Suggest ways for the students to record the items, for example, in columns with the English word on one side and the meaning and an example on the other, or as a mind-map with drawings in topic sections. Suggest also that students can revise words at home, by folding the page to hide one of the columns and remembering the word/meaning, or by drawing another, blank, mind-map and trying to fill it in.

Collages, posters and mobiles

Encourage the students to make posters, collages and mobiles with the language they are learning. For example, on the topic of appearances, they can cut out pictures from magazines and make a collage with them, writing descriptions of the people in English. Similarly, illustrated posters of grammar features can be made by the students (e.g. for regular and irregular forms such as plurals, verb forms, etc.). Not only do such displays make the walls look more attractive, but they provide a permanent reminder of the language in the classroom.

Dice and counters for games

For certain games in the book, dice and counters are needed. If you don't have them easily available, students can:

- cut small squares of paper and colour them to make counters; or write on them the numbers 1–6 and draw them from a bag instead of using dice

- scratch the numbers 1–6 on the sides of a hexagonal pencil, then roll it like a die to get a number.

Class management

Drilling techniques

Controlled, or restricted, language practice tasks should ideally be done at a brisk pace: this makes it more fun, as well as helping the students to produce the sounds more automatically. Here are some techniques to achieve this:

Choral (class) drilling

Once you have modelled and demonstrated the activity, use a 'large' circular gesture with your hands to indicate you want the whole class to answer. Insist on them speaking all together. Model the language at normal speed, and use quick hand gestures to keep up the speed of answering.

Individual drilling

Make sure the students can see your eyes, and indicate who you want to answer by making eye contact and an 'inviting' gesture with an open hand. With large classes you could move round the room and touch a student on the shoulder to indicate who should answer. Avoid using students' names, as it slows down the procedure.

Errors can be corrected on the spot in this kind of activity, using one of the following techniques:

- Repeat the sentence with the correct form, and get the whole class to repeat.
- Encourage other students to give the correct form.
- Indicate with a doubtful or questioning facial expression that there is an error.
- Repeat the sentence or phrase and stop before the error, eliciting the correct version.

Organizing pair and group work

Pair and group work offer students maximum opportunities to use their English. If the lesson is conducted entirely teacher–class, students will actually use their English very little. It may take your class some time to get used to this kind of work if they have never done it before, but if you persist, the benefits will soon be seen. If it is new for your class, begin with pair work for just a couple of minutes, and gradually extend the time spent in pairs each lesson. When students are happy with this, introduce groups of three, and later groups of four.

At the outset, explain the task and *demonstrate* how to do it, either with a student or by asking two students to demonstrate. Actually doing a bit of the task is the clearest way of telling students how to do it.

Always check that students have understood what to do before they start. You can ask questions which require a *yes/no* answer (e.g. *Are you going to write the answers?* or *either/or* questions (e.g. *Are you going to speak or write?*); or you can ask the students to raise their hands (e.g. *Who is A? Who is B?*). If the task is quite complex (e.g. a game), give the instructions in stages, and check understanding at each stage.

Encourage the students to face each other during the activity, either by turning round or by moving the seats to facilitate communication. If there is an odd student, put him/her with another pair or group.

Go round the class as soon as the students start working, to check that they are doing the activity

properly and to answer any queries. Also note down language errors. Don't correct at this point – it will distract the students and possibly inhibit them.

If you feel the noise level is too high, appoint someone in the group to be a 'noise monitor', who will be responsible for keeping the others' voices down if they get too excited.

If some students finish early, either ask them to add more words/sentences/questions to the task, or split them up and send them to work with other pairs or groups.

When giving feedback at the end of the activity, praise the students for their efforts. Using the notes you made during monitoring, choose the most important errors and either write them on the board or say them, without saying who made the error. Encourage students to try to correct the errors themselves. You may want to ask them to make a written note of the errors and the corrections in their notebooks.

Use of L1

With beginner classes, using L1 can often facilitate classroom procedures (e.g. for giving instructions or disciplining students). However, instruction-giving and informal interaction in the classroom provide opportunities for the use of English as a means of communication. Therefore it is advisable to try to phase out the use of L1 as soon as possible.

When giving instructions for tasks, always give the English first. Support understanding with gestures, mime and pictures from the book or your own drawings. Prepare flashcards with frequently-used phrases of classroom language written on (e.g. *Listen and point*, *What's the English word for . . .?*, *How do you spell . . .?*), illustrate them with drawings to show the meaning, and put them on the wall. They provide a quick reference for the students, and also a way of checking understanding: ask students to point at the correct flashcards when you give instructions.

Evaluating and assessing progress

Students' evaluation

Students are encouraged to assess and evaluate their own progress through the 'Think about it!' sections at the end of each unit and the 'Stop and think!' sections in each Revision unit.

Teacher's evaluation

Tests

There are 15 photocopiable tests in this Teacher's Book (Photocopiable pages 16–30), one for each teaching unit. Marks are out of a total of 20. An answer key is provided at the end of the Tests section.

Student profile

While tests will give an indication of the students' progress, they only indicate competence in certain areas of the syllabus. The student profile sheet on the following page will help you to build up a more complete picture of the students in your class. It will also provide you with a quick reference when you have to put together reports at the end of term.

Good luck, and enjoy teaching with *Brainwaves!*

Student profile

Student ....

Class ....

Teacher ....

Unit	Language				Skills work				Comments
	Grammar	Functional	Vocabulary	Pronunciation	Reading	Writing	Speaking	Listening	
1									
2									
3									
4									
5									
6									
7									
8									
9									
10									
11									
12									
13									
14									
15									

Tests (mark out of 20)

Test 1	Test 5	Test 9	Test 13 ....
Test 2	Test 6	Test 10	Test 14 ....
Test 3	Test 7	Test 11	Test 15 ....
Test 4	Test 8	Test 12	

General knowledge

Learning objectives

- expanding general knowledge
- talking about the animal world
- asking questions
- completing a quiz

Language focus

- *wh-* questions
- *how ...?* questions
- *yes/no* questions

Active vocabulary

alligator	bird	butterfly
camel	cheetah	chihuahua
crocodile	dolphin	eagle
elephant	far	galaxy
giraffe	heavy	How ...?
kilograms	kilometre	kiwi
land (*adjective*)	long	metres
polar bear	shark	Sun
tiger	tortoise	weigh
whale	Which ...?	

Receptive vocabulary

appropriate	blood	distance
fly (*verb*)	galaxy	general knowledge
height	intonation	Latin America
length	litre	nearly
pyramid	quiz	quizmaster
round (*noun*)	speed	the Milky Way
topic	travel (*verb*)	upside down
weight		

Materials

Reference material for Skills focus Exercise 6.

Copies of photocopiable page 1 for additional activity 6.

Lead-in

a Put students into groups and give them three minutes to write down the names of as many animals as they can. Groups take it in turns to say the animals on their list and get a point for any animal that no other group has thought of.

Vocabulary

(Student's Book page 4)

Exercises 1 and 2 ❶

- Do Lead-in a to activate students' animal vocabulary. Then ask them to give you an example of a land animal, a sea animal, a bird and an insect (they can use L1 if necessary). Now ask them to look at the photos on page 4: are there some animals here that were not mentioned in the lead-in?

- Put students into threes and see if they can say the names of any of these animals – in the labels, the first letter of each word is given to help them. Then ask them to complete all the labels by supplying the rest of the word from the list below. They can use their dictionaries for some of these if they need to.

- Play item 1 so that students can check their answers. Then replay it and ask them to repeat.

Answers

See Tapescript.

📼 TAPESCRIPT

1	camel	5	dolphin	9	tortoise
2	cheetah	6	kiwi	10	shark
3	chihuahua	7	tiger	11	blue whale
4	eagle	8	butterfly	12	giraffe

Exercise 2

- Keep students in their groups and ask them to put the animals into the correct groups. (Note that a tortoise could be classified as both a land and a sea animal.)

Answers

a   camel, cheetah, chihuahua, giraffe, tortoise, tiger

b   blue whale, dolphin, shark

c   eagle, kiwi

d   butterfly

Additional activity 1

Put students into groups and tell them to take it in turns to describe an animal without saying its name. The others in the group guess which animal is being described. Do an example with the whole class first.

Exercise 3

- Put students into pairs and ask them to discuss all they know about the animals in Exercise 1. They should use the present simple here, since they are talking about things that are generally true.

Exercise 4

- Students identify the four animals in the photos and match the questions with the answers under the photos. Point out that *How fast?* asks about speed, *How tall?* about height, *How long?* about length and *How heavy?* about weight. Check that students understand that we ask a person *How tall are you?* and not *How long are you?* (Height is measured vertically and length horizontally.)

▶ Note

Students may well have come across the word *high*. If they ask you about the difference between *high* and *tall*, here are a few guidelines:

- People and trees are *tall*. Buildings can sometimes be *tall*, too. Things that are a thin rectangular shape are generally *tall*.

- Things that are triangular or square-shaped are generally *high* (e.g. mountains). We also use *high* to talk about how far something is positioned above the ground. For example, a child standing on a chair is *higher* than his mother, but not *taller*.

Additional activity 2

Play 'Animal idioms'. The aim here is to enrich students' knowledge of vocabulary related to animals. Write this list on the board:

1 *butterflies*   2 *cats and dogs*
3 *whale*   4 *horse*   5 *pig*

Write the following sentences on the board. Put students into pairs and ask them to guess which animal goes into each gap.

a   *That's your third piece of cake! You're a ....!*

b   *The party yesterday was great fun – I really enjoyed it. I had a .... of a time!*

c   *I always feel nervous before a big test. I get .... in my stomach!*

d   *I'm really, really hungry. I could eat a ....!*

e   *It's raining a lot today! Look – it's raining ....*

The context should give students the definition of the idioms, but explain in L1 if necessary. Ask students if they can think of any equivalent idioms in their own language.

Answers: a 5; b 3; c 1; d 4; e 2

Language focus

(Student's Book page 77)

Exercises 1 and 2

- Divide students into groups and make sure they cover Exercise 2. Ask students to guess the answers to the questions. They are not expected to know the answers, of course, but the questions will provide interesting puzzles while familiarizing students with *How...?* questions. If you wish to turn this into a competition, tell students that they will get five points if they can guess any answer correctly.

- When students are ready, allow them to look at the answers in Exercise 2 and ask them to match these with the correct questions. Go through the answers with the whole class. Groups get one point for matching the correct answer to its question. Were any of the groups' original guesses right? You could give them some points if they were approximately right.

Answers

1 e 2 h 3 a 4 f 5 c 6 g 7 b 8 d

Focus

This section puts together the three different kinds of questions that students have met. The tense used here is the present simple, but the basic patterns are the same for the other tenses.

- Tell students to look at the underlined words in Exercise 1: these are all examples of *How ...?* questions. Some of these will already be familiar from Vocabulary Exercise 3. Put students into pairs and ask them to say when we use *How many?*, *How much?* and *How far?* Elicit example sentences for these. (*How many?* asks about quantity of plural [countable] nouns; *How much?* asks about quantity of singular [or uncountable] nouns; and *How far?* asks about distance.)

- Revise *wh-* questions by asking students to give you the question word we use when we want to ask about place (*Where*) or a thing (*What*, *Which*).

- The section on *yes/no* questions and answers is also revision. However, emphasize the point that the short answers use the first word of the question: <u>Can</u> polar bears swim? Yes, they <u>can</u>.

Exercise 3

- Ask students to work in pairs to complete the questions. Sometimes the gaps contain one word and sometimes two. This is quite a tricky exercise, so allow the pairs some time to think about it, and give help where needed. Check with the whole class to make sure they have the right questions before they go on to Exercise 4.

Answers

1 Where	4 What/Which	7 What
2 How many	5 Is	8 How much
3 Can/Do	6 Are	

Exercise 4

- Ask students where they can find the answers to these questions. Suggestions: in an encyclopaedia, in a science book, on a CD-ROM, on the Internet, from you, their parents or the science teacher. Give students a few days to find out as many answers as they can, before giving them the answers.

Answers

1 in the Arctic 2 eight 3 yes 4 a bat
5 yes 6 no 7 plankton 8 up to 270 kilos

Additional activity 3

If you think students will find it difficult to find the answers, or if you want to give them the answers in a different way, do the following. Write the answers on separate slips of paper, or photocopy them and cut the copy into slips (one set of answers per group of students). Working in groups, students have to match the answers with the questions in Exercise 3.

Skills focus

(Student's Book page 6)

Exercise 1

- Do Lead-in c to revise question forms. This will prepare students for the later exercises which ask them to write their own quiz questions.

- Ask students to look at the picture and say what is happening. Can they explain what a quiz is? (In the simplest form of quiz, a quizmaster asks questions and the contestants answer them.)

Additional activity 4

Tell students that you are going to hold a short quiz. Put students into teams and make sure they have their books shut. Tell them that the first team to answer a question correctly gets a point, and the winning team is the one with most points. You could ask students to think of animal names for their teams (e.g. 'The Dolphins', 'The Lion Lords', etc.). Ask a student to keep score, or write up the points on the board yourself.

Introduce the quiz in an authentic way (use the tapescript for language and ideas – in this way, you are previewing the listening that follows). Now ask students questions already to be found in this unit.

Exercise 2

- Put students into groups and ask them to think of possible questions for the answers on the three cards – in some cases, they might think of several possible questions. Tell them to use previous questions and the Focus examples to help them. Don't let them know which are the right questions at this stage – they will work this out when they do the quiz themselves in Exercise 4.

Exercise 3 ▣ ❷

- Ask students to listen to the quizmaster explaining about the quiz (remind them of the use of *have* to here). Ask them to go through the rules in their own words.

▣ TAPESCRIPT

Hello, and welcome to the Brainwaves Quiz Show. Let's begin straight away with – of course – round one. First, you just have to listen. I'll read all 12 questions. Then I'll read them again, one at a time, and you have to buzz if you know the answer. OK? Well, let's begin!

Exercise 4

- First put students into pairs, ask them to read through the questions and try to complete them. Each question matches an answer on the cards. Students decide which are the correct answers to their questions.

- Now put pairs together to make teams of four, and ask them to compare their questions and answers. If there is disagreement, they should discuss it together and come to some decision.

Exercise 5 ▣ ❸

- Students will now hear round one of the quiz. Play item 3, pausing to allow them time to correct their questions and to mark their answers with a tick or a cross. Play the tape again if necessary. Ask teams to add up their points and find out which team has won round one of the quiz.

▣ TAPESCRIPT

Quizmaster Round One. In this round I'm going to read the questions only. Think about the answers, but don't answer yet.

Question 1: Where are the pyramids?
Question 2: What is the smallest kind of dog?
Question 3: What is the biggest land animal?
Question 4: Which is the biggest country in Latin America?
Question 5: What is the name of our galaxy?
Question 6: Which is the biggest city in Turkey?
Question 7: How fast does light travel?
Question 8: How far away is the Sun?
Question 9: How much does an elephant weigh?
Question 10: Where is the Acropolis?
Question 11: How old is the Earth?
Question 12: What is the fastest animal on land?
Now I'm going to ask the questions again. You have five seconds to answer each question. Fingers on the buzzers, please. Ready?

Quizmaster Question 1. Where are the pyramids?

Emma In Giza, Egypt.

Quizmaster Correct! One point for Team A. Question 2. What is the smallest kind of dog?

Oliver The chihuahua.

Quizmaster Correct! Another point for Team A. Question 3. What is the biggest land animal?

Voice 1 The elephant.

Quizmaster Correct! One point for Team B. Question 4. Which is the biggest country in Latin America?

Oliver Peru?

Quizmaster No, I'm sorry that's not right. Can anyone from Team B give me the answer?

Voice 2 Brazil.

Quizmaster Correct! Another point for Team B! Question 5. What is the name of our galaxy?

Peter The Milky Way.

Quizmaster Correct! One point for Team A. Question 6. Which is the biggest city in Turkey?

Emma Istanbul.

Quizmaster Correct! Another point for Team A! So at the half-way point Team A has four points and Team B two points. Question 7. How fast does light travel?

Oliver Er … 300, 000 kilometres per second?

Quizmaster	Correct! And Team A gets another point! Question 8. How far away is the Sun?
Annette	About 100 million kilometres?
Quizmaster	No, I'm sorry that's not right. Team B?
Voice 1	It's 149 million kilometres!
Quizmaster	Absolutely correct! Question 9. How much does an elephant weigh?
Emma	About 5,000 kilograms.
Quizmaster	Correct! One point for Team A! Question 10. Where is the Acropolis?
Voice 2	Italy?
Quizmaster	No, I'm sorry, that's not right. Team A, can you answer?
Peter	Greece?
Quizmaster	Correct! One point for Team A. Question 11 How old is the Earth? … Nobody? Well, the correct answer is 4 thousand million years. Bad luck. No points that time. And now the last question for round one of the Whiz Kid competition. What is the fastest land animal on Earth?
Voice 2	The cheetah!
Quizmaster	Correct! And that's one point for Team B! Now let's look at the scores. At the end of round one, Team A has a total of 7 points, and Team B has 4 points. Congratulations, Team A!

Additional activity 5

Put students into pairs and ask them to look back at the questions in Language focus Exercise 3 and Skills focus Exercise 4. Referring to the Focus box, students work out which types of question they are.

- As suggested in the Speaking tip, ask students to listen again to the quizmaster in item 3 and pause the tape to let them repeat. Draw attention to the falling intonation in *Wh-* and *How* questions.

Additional activity 6

Pairwork quiz: Make enough copies of photocopiable page 1 for each pair in the class, and cut it into A and B parts. Students first work individually to try to find the matching quiz questions for their six answers. They then ask each other for the answers they don't have. If they find they have the same question for two different answers, they have to discuss the

information and use their general knowledge and common sense to find another question for one of the answers.

Correct combination of questions and answers:

1 Bc 2 Ab 3 Bf 4 Ad 5 Bb 6 Af
7 Ac 8 Be 9 Bd 10 Ae 11 Ba 12 Aa

Exercises 6 and 7

- Round two of the quiz will take some time to prepare. Still in their teams, students write their own quiz questions and answers (you should set a specific number, depending on the size of the class and the amount of time you want to spend on the activity). This may involve doing some research, so bring in reference material yourself, ask students to bring relevant books to the class and send individuals to the library to find out information if necessary. (Hint: get students to write some questions on subjects they study at school: History, Geography, Maths, etc.) The groups will need to discuss their material, decide on which questions to ask and make sure that the answers are accurate. Check each group's questions and answers.

- Groups take it in turn to read out their questions, identifying them clearly by number. They should say each question twice and then pause while students in the other groups consult together (quietly!) and decide what answer to write down. When all the questions have been asked, groups exchange answer sheets. In the same order as before, group representatives give the answers to the questions they set, and the groups mark each other's answers. The group with the highest number of points is the winner.

Exercise 8

- Ask the students to look at the picture. Go through the answers with the class. In groups, students discuss the questions. Listen to their ideas.

Exercise 9

- Go through the vocabulary on the page. Ask the students to tell you which subjects they like and don't like. Play the song.

Exercise 10

- Elicit the phrase *Don't know much about …* and write it on the board. In pairs, students make a list of subjects that they aren't good at and make their own version of the song. Listen to their songs. Have a class vote on which is the best.

○ **Think about it!**

These exercises are a basic round-up of the language taught in the unit. They can be done individually or in pairs in class, or for homework, then checked in the next lesson.

Answers

1 **1** shark **2** tortoise **3** cheetah **4** dolphin
2 **1** What do birds eat?
   2 How much does that man weigh?
   3 Where is Cape Town?
   4 How many people live in the Vatican City?
   5 How fast can Concorde fly?
3 **1** No, they can't. **2** Yes, they do.
   3 No, they haven't.
4 *Students' own answers*

Workbook answers

❶

a 5 **b** 3 **c** 6 **d** 2 **e** 8 **f** 7 **g** 9 **h** 1 **i** 10
j 4

❷

2 What job does he do?
3 What kind of car has he got?
4 What is his wife's name?
5 What does she do?
6 What is their furniture like?
7 What do you think of them?

❸

3 What film did you watch last night?
4 Where does Harry live?
5 4
6 What time is it?
7 4
8 What time did you go to bed?
9 Who invented the television?
10 What (job) does your father do?
11 What did they have for lunch yesterday?
12 4

❹

2 How tall is he?
3 How much does he weigh?
4 How fast can he run?
5 – How old is she?
     – She's 18.
6 – How tall is she?
     – She's 160 cm.
7 – How much does she weigh?
     – She weighs 85 kg.
8 – How far can she throw the javelin?
     – She can throw the javelin 48 m.

❺

3 No, it doesn't.   **6** No, they don't.
4 Yes, it is.   **7** Yes, it can.
5 No, they haven't.   **8** Yes, it has.

❻

1 How **2** Where **3** Are **4** Have **5** Do **6** Do
7 Why **8** When

❼ *Students' own answers*

❽ *Students' own answers*

Flick back!

• cheetah, tiger, lion
• chihuahua
• skull
• bald

Buzz words

Across: 1 distance **4** kilo **7** nine **8** height **9** far
     10 many **11** fast **14** length **16** long
     17 metre

Down: 1 do **2** speed **3** centimetres **4** kg
     5 litres **6** heavy **11** forty **12** tall **13** weigh
     15 are

What's in a dish?

Learning objectives

- talking about food
- talking about recipes and ingredients
- cross-cultural cooking
- giving instructions

Language focus

- limited use of present simple passive
- imperatives for instructions

Active vocabulary

beef	chillies	corn
covered	cream	dish (= meal)
equipment	filled	fish
flour	fork	fruit
garlic	lettuce	made with
mayonnaise	meat	milk
mushrooms	onions	recipe
rice	salad	served
spices	sugar	tomato
tuna	vegetables	

Receptive vocabulary

butter	calzone	cook (*verb*)
cucumber	curry	dairy products
delicious	equipment	glorious
grain	hard boiled eggs	Home Economics
ingredients	inside	mash
mixing bowl	mixture	omelette
roll (bread)	shell	soy sauce
spread	spring rolls	tablespoon
tacos	teaspoon	toothpicks

Materials

Copies of instructions for Additional activity 6.

Copies of photocopiable page 2 for Additional activity 8.

Lead-ins

a   This revises animal vocabulary from Unit 1. Put students into big groups and ask them to take it in turns to mime an animal (they must not speak while doing this). The others guess which animals is being mimed.

b   Put students into threes. Give them five minutes to find three kinds of food that they all like eating and three foods that they all hate. Then ask each group to report their likes and dislikes to the rest of the class.

c   Put students into groups and ask them to say where they think these dishes come from and what is in them: curry, spring rolls, calzone, tacos, guacomole, paella, sushi, haggis, shortbread, milk shake. The first four are mentioned in this unit. Guacomole comes from Mexico and is made of mashed avocados; paella – Spain, made of rice, seafood and chicken; sushi – Japan, rice rolls with raw fish or cucumber; haggis – Scotland, made of sheep's stomach; shortbread – UK (Scottish shortbread is well-known), biscuit made with flour, butter and sugar; milk shake – USA, milk, ice cream and fruit blended together to make a drink.

Vocabulary

(Student's Book page 8)

- For revision of animal vocabulary from Unit 1, do Lead-in a.

Exercises 1 and 2 🔊 ❶

- Do Lead-in b.
- Give students time to work individually to match the food words and pictures. They should be able to work out most words by a process of deduction, but if there are some they are not sure of, they should leave the gap blank.
- Now put students into threes to check their answers and see if their partners can help them fill their blanks.
- Play item 1 so that students can check their answers. Play the tape again and ask them to repeat.

Answers

2 cream   3 milk   4 cheese   6 tuna   7 chicken
9 potatoes   10 lettuce   11 onions
12 mushrooms   14 rice   15 flour   17 spices
18 sugar

🔊 TAPESCRIPT

1 eggs   2 cream   3 milk   4 cheese   5 beef
6 tuna   7 chicken   8 tomatoes   9 potatoes
10 lettuce   11 onions   12 mushrooms   13 corn
14 rice   15 flour   16 oil   17 spices   18 sugar

Exercise 3

- Students should now be able to guess what *dairy products* and *grains* mean from the examples given. Explain in L1 if necessary. Divide your class into five groups and ask them to add more words to each of the food categories. Advise them to think of products from their own country as examples. Go round giving help, translating from L1 if necessary.
- Nominate a group for each category and ask representatives to come to the board all together and write their words for that category. When they have finished, the representatives can stay at the board and add words (or corrections) suggested by other groups. Give the class plenty of time to copy down the lists and ask you any questions.

Additional activity 1

Put students into groups and ask them to tell each other which of the food items on page 8 they eat every day, twice a week, every week, sometimes or never.

Exercises 4 and 5

- Tell students what your favourite dish is and what ingredients you need to make it. This provides students with a model of what to do, as well as pre-teaching the word *ingredients*. In pairs or threes, students talk about the ingredients needed for the three dishes in the pictures. Now ask them to tell each other what their favourite dish is and what ingredients they need to make it.

Additional activity 2

Pre-teach *delicious* and *disgusting*. Put students into groups of four and tell them to decide on two delicious ingredients and two disgusting ones. Ask them to write these four items on a piece of paper. Underneath, they should write: *milk, eggs, flour, tomatoes, oil*. They then pass their paper on to the next group, who have to devise a new dish using all the ingredients in the list. Groups should give their dish a name. When students are ready, ask them to walk around the class telling and asking each other about their dishes. Who invented the most creative/ disgusting/delicious dish?

Language focus

(Student's Book page 9)

Exercise 1

- Do Lead-in c, but don't give students the answers to the first four food items (spring rolls, curry, tacos or calzone) as these are dealt with in this section.
- Put students into pairs and ask them to answer the questions. Ask students to guess where the children are from and what they are making.

Exercise 2

- Ask students to read the ingredients and make sure that they understand all of them. Ask them to find the picture of spring rolls and use the table to say what you need to make them.

Exercise 3 🔊 ❷

- Make sure students cover the dialogues in Exercise 6. Talk about your favourite dish, saying how it is made, what it is filled with and how it is served, in order to pre-teach *filled* and *served*. Play item 2 and ask students to answer the questions.

Answers

a flour

b meat, mushrooms and vegetables

c soy sauce or chilli sauce

 TAPESCRIPT

Dialogue 1

Oliver What are these?

Girl They're spring rolls. They're made with flour. They're filled with meat, mushrooms and vegetables. They're served with soy sauce or chilli sauce.

Exercise 4 ❸

• Before playing item 3, ask students to refer to the photos and guess what ingredients can be found in curry, tacos and calzone. Then play the tape and ask students to complete the table in Exercise 2. Ask students to check their answers with each other before replaying the tape.

Answers

curry: meat, vegetables, onions, garlic, spices

tacos: corn, meat, tomatoes, onions, chillies, garlic

calzone: flour, meat, mushrooms, tomatoes, cheese

 TAPESCRIPT

Dialogue 2

Oliver What's this?

Boy It's curry. It's made with meat, vegetables, onions, garlic, and lots of spices. It's served with rice. Be careful, it's hot – but very tasty!

Dialogue 3

Oliver What are these?

Boy They're tacos. Tacos are made with corn. They're filled with meat, tomatoes, onions, chillies and garlic. Here, have some.

Dialogue 4

Oliver What's this funny bread?

Girl It's not bread, it's an Italian pizza. It's called calzone and it's made with flour. It's filled with meat, mushrooms, tomatoes, and cheese. It's delicious! Don't touch it – I have to cook it first!

Oliver Oh, sorry!

Focus

• Introduce students to this particular passive expression. The intention here is not to deal with

the passive in depth, but if students want to know more about the structure you could show that it is formed by subject + *be* + past participle, and explain that the past participle of most verbs is the same as the past simple. Elicit the full forms of *It's* and *They're* (*It is, They are*).

• Put the students into pairs or threes. Ask them to say what the dishes are made with, filled with and served with, referring to the table of ingredients and remembering what was said in the dialogues. You could also ask them to look back at the pictures in Vocabulary Exercise 4 and to suggest what these three dishes are made with and served with.

• Ask the class to think of dishes from their country or region. Ask them to use passive expressions to talk about each dish:

This dish is called …
It's filled with …
It's covered with …
It's served with …

Additional activity 3

Tell students that they are going to design a menu – with a difference! Write the following on the board:

Rita's Revolting Restaurant

Starters
Slug Surprise – This is made with big fat slugs and served with strawberry jam.

Main Courses
Cat Soup – This delicious soup is covered with old toe nails for extra taste.

Desserts
Cockroach Crunch – This is chocolate cake filled with cockroaches and served with hot chilli mayonnaise.

Put students into groups and ask them to design their own revolting menu, using the same headings. Remind them to invent a name for their dish and then write a description of it. Check students' writing, then ask them to write out their menus neatly, with illustrations if they wish. Display the menus on the wall and give students time to walk around and read each other's.

Exercises 5 and 6

• Put students into pairs and ask them to read the dialogues. They should use the ingredients table to complete the gaps. Then play item 3 again, pausing where necessary to give students time to check and correct their answers.

Answers

1   1 flour   2 meat   3 mushrooms
    4 vegetables

2   1 meat   2 vegetables   3 onions   4 spices

3   1 corn   2 meat   3 onions   4 chillies
    5 garlic

4   1 flour   2 meat   3 mushrooms   4 cheese

Additional activity 4

Play one or two of the dialogues again and ask students to listen and repeat. Concentrate on pronunciation and intonation.

Additional activity 5

Put students into groups and ask each group to write ten words from the unit in large letters. However, they should split up the word so that some of the letters are on one piece of paper and some on another; for example, MEL / ON or AP / PLE. Students mix up the pieces of paper. They then swap with another group and try to make the complete words.

○ Skills focus

(Student's Book page 10)

Exercises 1 and 2 ▣ ❹

- Students look at the pictures and name any ingredients they can recognize. Ask them to guess what the teacher is doing/making – however, this will be rather a puzzle at this stage, as the photos are jumbled.

- Elicit the meaning of *recipe*, and ask students to read the list of ingredients in the recipe for 'Mayonnaise Monsters'. Draw their attention to the Listening tip. Can they guess what words – or what kinds of words – might fit in the blanks? Play item 4, pausing if necessary. Go through the answers and write them on the board so that students' spelling is correct. Make sure they understand the difference between *teaspoon* and *tablespoon*.

Answers

bread, eggs, butter, 2, mayonnaise, salt, pepper

▣ TAPESCRIPT

This is our second lesson on party food, and today we're making Mayonnaise Monsters. Mayonnaise Monsters are sandwiches filled with egg mayonnaise. Now let's see what we need. We need six bread rolls, four hard-boiled eggs, a teaspoon of butter, two tablespoons of mayonnaise, a tablespoon of ketchup, salt and pepper.

Exercise 3

- Students look at the pictures to find the items in the 'Equipment' list. Ask them to say what they can be used for. This will give you a chance to pre-teach the verbs *cut, mix* and *mash*.

Exercises 4 and 5 ▣ ❺

- In pairs, students guess the correct order of the pictures. Then ask them to listen to item 5 and check their answers. For this, they don't need to understand every word on the tape but should try to get a general grasp of what is happening at each step.

- Now ask students, still in their pairs, to read the recipe instructions and to guess the missing words. They now have a lot of evidence to help them – the pictures, the lists of ingredients and equipment, and the other words in the text itself. Play the tape again, pausing if necessary to allow them to correct or write in the words. Check answers with the whole class.

Answers

1 eggs   2 mixing bowl   3 mayonnaise, salt, pepper   4 ketchup   5 knife   6 olives, toothpicks

▣ TAPESCRIPT

To make Mayonnaise Monsters, first take the shells off the eggs. Put the eggs in the mixing bowl and mash them with the fork. Mix in the butter. Then add the mayonnaise, salt and pepper and mix well. Add the ketchup to make the mixture pink. When you have finished, cut the rolls in half with a knife and spread the mixture inside. Make the faces with olives, pieces of carrot and cucumber. Use toothpicks to keep them in place.

Photocopy or write out the following recipe instructions for making Honey Banana Milk Shake, and cut them up, so that each step is on a separate piece of paper. You need one set of instructions for each group.

Instructions
Peel and cut the banana into the liquidizer.
Add the milk, honey and ice cream.
Put the lid on and mix, using the low speed.
Then mix on high speed for a few seconds.
Pour the milk shake into the tall glasses.
Enjoy!

Dictate (or write on the board) these lists of ingredients and equipment:

Ingredients
1 ripe banana
1/2 pint (250 ml) cold milk
1 tablespoon honey
1 big scoop of ice cream

Equipment
Electric liquidizer
2 tall glasses

Divide your class into groups, give them the instructions and ask them to put them into the correct order.

Exercise 6

- Ask students to look at their completed recipes for Mayonnaise Monsters. The verbs used to give instructions are in the imperative: we form this from the infinitive without *to*. Remind students to use the imperative (not 'You put/add' etc.) when they write their own instructions.

- In groups, students write a list of ingredients and a simple recipe. Encourage them to be inventive in the sandwiches they create! They can use the ingredients they have learnt in this unit and come up with some imaginative combinations!

- Check students' writing. Then ask them to circulate, telling and asking each other about their sandwich recipes.

Students ask someone at home how to make their favourite dish and write a rough draft of a recipe for you to correct. Then ask them to write their recipes out neatly and include drawings if they like. Collect these and their sandwich recipes and put them into a folder to create your class's very own recipe booklet. If you are able to make multiple photocopies of the recipes, every student can have their own copy.

Pairwork: this activity increases cultural awareness, as well as practising language used for food and eating. Make copies of photocopiable page 2, enough for one per pair of students. In their pairs, students discuss the statements about British eating habits, and decide if they think they are true (*T*) or false (*F*). If they answer *F*, they should give reasons. As they go through the statements, ask them to compare the eating habits of their own country. Finally, talk about these questions in a discussion with the whole class.

Answers
1 F (They don't say anything.) 2 F 3 T
4 T 5 F 6 T 7 F 8 F (They usually eat earlier, between 6 and 7.30 in the evening.)
9 T 10 F 11 T 12 F

⊙ Food, glorious food

Exercise 1

- Elicit the names of the dishes. Say the names in random order and ask students to call out the letters of the corresponding pictures. Then say the letters and ask them to call out the names.

- In pairs, students remind each other of the main ingredients in each of the dishes. They can refer back to Exercises 2 and 6 if they are not sure.

Exercises 2, 3 and 4

- Ask students to fill in the blank squares with the names of two dishes from their country. Ask them to think about what the dish is made with and how it is served.

- In small groups, students follow the instructions and play the game.

○ Think about it!

These exercises are a basic round-up of the language taught in the unit. They can be done individually or in pairs in class, or for homework, then checked in the next lesson.

Answers

1 **2** bowl **3** fork **4** lettuce **5** pieces
6 tomatoes **7** mayonnaise **8** garlic **9** tuna

2 and 3 *Students' own answers*

Workbook answers

❶

1 lettuce (d)	**4** mushroom (h)	**7** potato (g)
2 tomato (e)	**5** apple (c)	**8** orange (i)
3 banana (f)	**6** carrot (b)	**9** onion (a)

❷

Across: 2 tuna **5** cheese **6** egg **7** milk **8** cream
Down: 1 butter **3** beef **4** yoghurt **5** chicken

❸

1 salt **2** pepper **3** garlic **4** corn **5** rice
6 sugar

❹ *(Possible answers)*

2 It's (a) curry. It's made with meat/vegetables, onions, garlic and spices.

3 It's an omelette. It's made with eggs and butter.

4 It's a spring roll. It's made with flour and vegetables.

5 It's a pizza. It's made with flour, tomatoes and cheese.

6 It's a salad. It's made with lettuce and other vegetables.

❺

1 served with bread
2 is made with tuna, onions, rice and corn
3 filled with beef and vegetables
4 It's served with fries or rice
5 made with
6 with vegetables and chips
7 served with boiled potatoes and vegetables
8 served with cream

❻

1 one **2** 500 grams **3** minced beef **4** tomatoes and kidney beans **5** at the end / after 50 minutes
6 boiled rice

❼ *Students' own answers*

Stunning stunts!

Learning objectives

- talking about doing dangerous things
- learning about stunts
- talking about plans or intentions

Language focus

- *have to*
- *going to* future (intentions)

Active vocabulary

barrel	building	cliff
dive	fall off	flames
fly	hang	jetski
jump out of	motorcycle	pilot
plane	roof	stunt
wing (of plane)		

Receptive vocabulary

action	based on	caption
certain	clearly	dare devil
edge	exact	future
intention	lip	noise
planned	ramp	scared
sequence	signal	situation
slowly	stunning	velocity

Materials

Copies of photocopiable page 3 for Additional activity 7.

Lead-ins

a Put students into groups and ask them to write the name of a food or drink for each letter of the alphabet.

b Write *Stunning Stunts* on the board. Give examples of where students can see stunts – in a James Bond film (or an equivalent in your country), in action films, computer games, comics, etc. Ask students to tell each other what kind of stunts the stuntmen and women do, using these words: *fly, jump, swim, fall off, land, plane, jetski, parachute, cliff, motorbike.*

c Ask students if they have any plans for the future. Ask them *What are you going to do or be when you are older?* They could talk about this in pairs, and then take it in turns to give you a sentence saying what they are going to do or be.

Vocabulary

(Student's Book page 12)

- To revise food vocabulary from Unit 2, do Lead-in a.

Exercise 1

- Do Lead-in b. This will start students thinking about stunts and related vocabulary.

- Put students into small groups and ask them to say what they can see in the pictures and what they think is happening. This revises the present continuous tense while also giving students time to study the pictures and activate vocabulary.

- Now ask students to look at the phrases and match them with the different parts of the stunt. They should write the numbers in the boxes provided.

Answers

2 jump into the plane

3 land on the motorcycle

4 fall off the motorcycle

5 dive into the sea

6 walk to the edge of the roof

7 fly through the flames

8 ride up the bridge

9 hold on to the edge of the cliff

10 swim under water

11 jump out of the plane

12 jump over the train

13 climb down the cliff

14 get on to the jetski

Exercise 2 ❶

- Play item 1 and ask students to check their answers.

📼 TAPESCRIPT

First, Kevin has to climb up the building. Then he has to walk to the edge of the roof and jump into the plane. Then he has to fly through the flames, jump out of the plane and land on the motorcycle. After that, he has to ride up the bridge and jump over the train. Then he has to fall off the motorcycle, hold on to the edge of the cliff, climb down the cliff and dive into the sea. Finally, he has to swim under water and get on to the jetski.

Exercise 3

- Put students into groups and ask them to brainstorm possible scenarios and activities for stunts; for example, on a train, in a burning building, an earthquake, hang-gliding, scuba-diving etc. Using their own scenarios or different combinations from the pictures in the book, students invent their own stunt sequence. They should think of at least five different parts for the stunt, and to decide what Kevin has to do in each part. Encourage them to make their stunts creative and exciting.

Additional activity 1

Put students into small groups and tell them that they are film directors shooting an exciting new action film. They are going to use some of the stunts they invented in Exercise 3 in their new film. Unfortunately, the film set is very noisy, so they must mime their stunts to the stuntmen and stuntwomen. Groups take it in turns to be the directors and mime the stunts they have decided on. The class has to guess what the stunts are. Give the groups time to rehearse their mimes before asking them to perform in front of the class.

Additional activity 2

Tell students that the stunt sequence with Kevin on page 12 is the end of a film. Put students into groups and ask them to come up with a storyline. Who is Kevin? What happened before this stunt, and why? Who are the good and the bad guys? Ask students to give their film a name. Now ask them to circulate and tell each other about the content of their films.

Language focus

(Student's Book page 13)

Exercises 1 and 2 📼 ❷

- Ask students to look at the pictures on this page and guess what *dare devil* means. Ask the students if any of them would like to do stunts when they are older. Why/Why not?

- Do Lead-in c. Don't worry if students do not get the grammar correct. This lead-in presents *going to*. It also acts as a diagnostic tool to tell you whether students are familiar with this structure or have never met it before.

- Ask students to discuss the questions in Exercise 1 in pairs. Then play item 2 and ask them to check their answers. Use this as a chance to set the scene for the next part of the listening.

Answers

a a stuntman **b** a TV or radio interviewer
c barrels

🔲 TAPESCRIPT

Anneka Welcome, everybody, to *Incredible but True!* coming to you today from Fairfield Airfield. I'm Anneka Price, and I'm going to introduce you to some amazing people. Have we got an incredible show lined up for you today! Are you ready?

Our first *Incredible but True!* performer is David Acton. David is an experienced stuntman and his favourite stunt is the one he's going to do today. David, Hello, How are you?

David Fine, thanks, Anneka.

Anneka So what are you going to do today, David?

David Well, I'm going to do a stunt with my motorcycle and a lot of barrels.

Anneka And is that one of the barrels there?

David Yes, of course.

Exercise 3 🔲 ❸

- Ask students to say what they think is going to happen next. What stunt is David Acton going to perform? Put students into pairs and ask them to guess the answers to the questions. Play item 3, pausing where necessary to allow students to complete the sentences. Go through the answers with them, making sure that they recognize the dangers involved in this stunt.

🔲 TAPESCRIPT

Anneka So, how many of these barrels are you going to jump over?

David I'm going to jump over seventy-five barrels.

Anneka 75? Wow! That's a lot of barrels! And this is going to be a first for you isn't it?

David Yes, Anneka. And not just for me. It's going to be a new world record.

Anneka And that's not all, is it?

David No, it isn't. To make it more difficult, I'm going to set fire to the barrels first.

Anneka Set fire to them? Wow! Tell me, David just how difficult is this stunt?

David It's very difficult, Anneka. I need to reach a speed of 160 kilometres per hour.

Anneka Amazing.

David And when I jump, I'm going to be ten metres off the ground.

Anneka You're going to jump 10 metres?

David Ten metres high, yes. I need to jump 30 metres to get over all 75 barrels.

Anneka David, what can I say? You're amazing. Good luck!

Exercise 4

- Ask students *What is going to happen? Will David be successful?* Tell them they are going to listen to Anneka as she watches the stunt. How do they think she feels? Play item 4.

- Replay the tape and pause at *he isn't going to jump high enough.* Ask the students what is happening. What can Anneka see?

🔲 TAPESCRIPT

Anneka For those of you who have just tuned in, today on *Incredible but True!* stunt man David Acton going to set a new world record! David's just putting on his helmet and getting on to his motorbike. He's going to ride around the race track first. He needs to reach an incredible 160 kilometres per hour to jump the barrels.

He's starting to race around the track now. And they're setting fire to the barrels … it looks very dangerous. David's going to jump over 75 barrels in all. If he does it, he'll set a new world record.

He's coming up to the ramp now. Is he going fast enough? … Oh no. He isn't going to jump high enough … but he's in the air … the bike looks too low … is he going to do it? … yes! And it's a new world record!

He's looking back at the jump now. He can't believe he did it! Congratulations David!

Focus

- Look at the sentence *He's going to jump over the barrels* and ask if this refers to the past, the present or the future. Ask *Is David sure about this?* Point out the barrels set up in the picture and elicit the point that it is a firm plan or intention. Make it clear that *He's = He is*, and get students to work out the structure we use to talk about future intentions: verb *be* + *going to* + infinitive.

- Return to the example *He isn't going to jump high enough* and again make it clear that this refers to the future. Elicit that Anneka is sure about this – she has the evidence in front of her!

- Referring to this example, ask students to say how the negative of *going to* is formed (the negative of *be + going to*). Ask students to put the other sentences in the Focus box into the negative form. Change the subject from *He* to *They* – what are the sentences now, and what are the negatives?

Additional activity 3

Students have practised making questions in Unit 1, so should be familiar with the inverted word order of questions with the verb *be*. Ask students to write the question form for the examples in the Focus box. Then give them some other examples using different pronouns.

Exercise 5

- Ask students to say where the people in the picture are and what they are going to do next. Now write the names of the objects in the pictures on the board (e.g. *bungee jumping*, *diving board*, *skydivers*, *parachutes*) and ask students to identify them in the pictures.

Additional activity 4

Put students into pairs and ask them to conduct an interview based on one of the pictures. Student A is the interviewer and B is one of the 'Dare Devils', and they are talking about the activity before it begins. A asks questions about what B is going to do, and B replies. Students can then choose a new picture and exchange roles.

Additional activity 5

Put the students into pairs and ask them to look at Kevin's stunts on page 14. One student is the stunt co-ordinator and the other is a cameraman/woman in Kevin's film, and they are discussing what he is going to do. Students can explain and ask questions in these roles while you monitor and help where necessary.

Skills focus

(Student's Book page 14)

Terminal Velocity

Background

Terminal Velocity is an American action film starring Charlie Sheen.

Exercises 1 and 2

- Students look at the two pictures on the left-hand side of the page and say what is happening in each picture. Use this to pre-teach appropriate vocabulary. Then ask students to read the clues and predict how Ditch is going to get from one plane to the other.

- Then ask students to look at the pictures and match the clues (not full sentences yet) with the correct pictures. Make sure you point out that the pictures are in the wrong order. Give students a chance to revise their prediction about how Ditch is going to do the stunt.

Answers

a	climb on the wing	d sit on the wing
b	stand on the wing	e hang by the legs
c	turn the plane over	

Exercise 3 🔊 ❺

- Students look at the pictures and listen to item 5 to put them into the correct order.

Answers

1 d   2 b   3 e   4 a   5 c

🔊 TAPESCRIPT

Ditch Stop! Stop! Stop! Lower! Slower!

Pilot What do you think you're doing?

Ditch All right. Listen to me now. I'm going to climb out on to the wing. When I get stable. I'm going to give you a signal. Then you're going to turn this plane over.

Pilot What? Upside-down?

Ditch Yeah.

Pilot No problem!

Ditch I'm going to hang by my legs from the wing …

Pilot What? With the plane upside down? You're crazy, man.

Ditch Then you're going to turn the plane back over, right side up. Then I'm going to be sitting on the top wing. That way, when you fly near the other plane, …

Pilot You mean, I'm going to fly right next to that plane there?

Ditch Yep, that's right. You're going to fly next to the other plane. Then I'm going to climb up the ramp and into the plane. You got that?

Pilot So I'm going to fly near the plane, and you're going to climb into it. Are you out of your mind?

Ditch Yes. Yes, I am.

- Now ask students to expand their clues into full sentences, using *going to*. Make sure they recognize that it is the pilot (not Ditch) who is going to turn the plane over.

Exercises 4

- Put students into pairs or threes and tell them that in all the sentences Ditch is talking to the pilot. Ask them to guess which words go into the blanks. Sometimes there is one word missing and sometimes two.

- Replay item 5 and give students time to check their guesses. Go through the answers with the whole class.

Answers	
a going, climb	e going to, plane
b going, give	f I'm, sitting
c you're, over	g going to fly
d hang, wing	h going to

Exercise 5

- Write the first word of each of the pilot's questions on the board as a guide, and ask students to try to remember or work out what his questions were. Play item 5 again, pausing if necessary for students to write the questions. Elicit answers and write the correct words on the board.

Additional activity 6

You can do Exercises 4 and 5 as a jigsaw listening, if circumstances allow. Divide the class into two (A and B). Send Group A to the library or a free room and set them some work to do. With Group B, play item 5 and ask them to write down Ditch's words. Then send this group out of the room and call back Group A. Play the tape and ask them to make a note of the pilot's questions. Then go on to Exercise 6.

Exercise 6

- Ask students to use the notes they wrote for Exercises 4 and 5 to help them act out the

dialogue between Ditch and the pilot. Once students have gone through the dialogue once, ask them to do it again – this time concentrating on pronunciation and intonation.

Additional activity 7

Pairwork: Make enough copies of photocopiable page 3 for each pair in the class and cut it into A and B parts. Students have different pictures from an action film sequence. Students take it in turns to describe the action in their pictures, while their partner asks questions and makes notes in the appropriate frame. When they are both clear about the content of all the pictures, they have to decide together what the correct order of the pictures is.

Answer
Correct order: 8, 4, 11, 1, 5, 9, 7, 3, 12, 2, 10, 6

Additional activity 8

Put students into groups and tell that they are the scriptwriters for *Terminal Velocity*. Ask them to write out the plot of the film, using these questions to help them:

Why does Ditch want to get into the plane?
What's going to happen if he can't?
Who is on the plane?
Where is the woman? Is he going to rescue her?
What's going to happen on the plane?
What's going to happen at the end of the film?

Ask each group to report their ideas. Tell them about the actual plot and ending of the film. Which do they prefer: their own stories or the real one? If possible, show students the stunt sequence on video.

Trapped!

Exercises 7 and 8

- With the whole class, look at the picture and discuss the questions. Elicit as many ideas as possible and jot them down on the board under two headings: *What is happening?* and *What is going to happen?* Use these two categories to make students aware of the difference between the present continuous and *going to*.

Exercise 9

- Start this exercise by setting up an example scenario where someone is trapped, using a location that everyone knows in the school. For example:

You are in the science lab and you are finishing some work. Suddenly you hear someone outside the door – it's the science teacher and she is laughing! You go to the door, but you can't open it – it's locked. Under the door you see yellow smoke – it's coming into the lab. It smells horrible! You run to the window but you can't open it. The lab is full of smoke and you feel sick. What are you going to do?

Elicit suggestions – as many as possible.

- In pairs, students think of their own scenario and then work out a plan for escape, using *going to*. Encourage them to use their imagination to make their plan as ingenious as possible!

Exercise 10

- With the whole class, ask pairs to take it in turns to describe the situation in which they are trapped. The others have to ask them questions, as in the example, to work out their escape plan.

◉ Think about it!

These exercises are a basic round-up of the language taught in the unit. They can be done individually or in pairs in class, or for homework, then checked in the next lesson.

Answers

1 1   2   3   4
2 1 Jake is going to jump into the river.
   2 Anna and Maria are going to fall into the swimming pool.
   3 I'm going to climb the mountain.
   4 The girls are going to get off the bus.

Workbook answers

❶
1 parachute 2 bridge 3 train 4 cliff 5 jetski
6 barrel 7 roof 8 wing

❷
2 She is going to dive into the barrel.
3 He is going to land in the river.
4 She is gong to climb down the ladder.
5 They are going to jump on to the train.
6 He is going to ride through the flames.

❸
2 isn't going to run
3 aren't going to sleep
4 I'm not going to cook
5 you're not going to get on well
6 aren't going to get married

❹
1 I'm going to play tennis
2 Are you going to visit Uncle Jack
3 I'm going to buy
4 I'm not going to go
5 I'm going to stay
6 I'm going to cook dinner
7 are you going to do
8 I'm going to watch a football match

❺
2 Is she going to buy a car?
   No, she's going to buy a motorbike.
3 Are they going to watch a volleyball match?
   No, they're going to watch a tennis match.
4 Is he going to be a postman?
   No, he's going to be a policeman.
5 Is she going to feed the dog?
   No, she's going to feed the cat.

❻
3 She's going to climb up a cliff.
4 She's going to dive from the clifftop into the sea.
5 She isn't going to swim to the bottom of the sea.
6 She isn't going to jump from a moving train.
7 She's going to ride a motorbike into a wall.
8 She isn't going to hang upside-down from a plane.
9 She's going to fight with a tiger.
10 She isn't going to slip on a banana skin.

❼
1 Stan 2 Jane 3 Sue 4 Frank 5 Stan 6 Sue

❽ *Students' own answers*

Buzz words

Across: 3 happy **5** bald **7** rice **8** cheetah
  9 shell **11** beef **12** fork
Down: 1 speed **2** mash **4** went **6** cheese
  7 roof **8** cliffs **10** early

It's showtime!

Learning objectives

- comparing past and present
- talking about theatres and shows
- learning about different kinds of theatre

Language focus

- present simple contrasted with past simple
- irregular past forms

Active vocabulary

audience	ballet	conductor
mask	movements	musical (*noun*)
nowadays	orchestra	perform
performers	rock concert	scenery
speak lines	stage	theatre
wear		

Receptive vocabulary

altogether	angry	believe
burn	cast	chorus
contrast	cry	exactly
excitement	female	forest
hero	live (*adjective*)	make-up
movement	open-air	playwright
presentation	remind	rich
same	teenage	traditional

Lead-ins

a Put students into groups and ask them to look at the title of this unit. Ask them to decide what it means and what the unit will probably be about. Where can you see shows? Indoors? Outdoors? Do students usually go to see shows – if so, where and what? Is there a show that they really want to see at the moment? Where is it and why do they want to see it?

b This is a lead-in related to the song. Ask students: *Do you have street parties or celebrations in the streets in your country? Describe them. Why do people have parties in the street? What do they do? Which countries are famous for having street festivals?* Students can discuss these questions in groups. Ask them to imagine they are going to have a street party. They should decide on food, music, activities and costumes.

Materials

Copies of photocopiable page 4 for Additional activity 7.

Extra material relating to Shakespeare for project work, Additional activity 8.

Extra material about traditional kinds of theatre in your country for Skills focus Exercise 9.

Vocabulary

(Student's Book page 16)

Exercises 1 and 2

- Do Lead-in a to get students thinking about shows and the theatre. Ask students to use the words in the wordbank to complete the labels. Then play item 1 so that students can check their answers.

- Play the tape again and ask students to listen and repeat.

Answers

See Tapescript.

TAPESCRIPT

1	audience	5	orchestra	8	lights
2	seats	6	actress	9	dancer
3	stage	7	actor	10	conductor
4	scenery				

Additional activity 1

Write these words on the board and ask students to say or guess what they are.

dressing room   box office   usher/usherette
backstage
box   row

Answers
dressing room – place where actors and actresses get dressed and put on their make-up
box office – place where you buy your tickets
usher/usherette – person who shows you to your seat
backstage – the area behind the stage which the audience cannot see
box – private balcony with 4–6 seats only
row – a line of seats

Exercises 3 and 4

- Ask students to look at the photographs and say what is happening / what they can see. Ask them to match the shows in the photos with the words in the list.

- Put students into small groups and ask them and to think of other shows they know that fit into these categories. They should tell each other which of these kinds of show they like and dislike, and why. When did they last see a show and what was it?

Exercise 5

- Still in their groups, students choose one kind of show from Exercise 3 and describe what the performers do. The present simple is the tense they should use here, for things which happen regularly or always.

Exercise 6

- Give students about five minutes to think of as many different types of phrases as they can using the three verbs. Alternatively, you could choose to make this into a competition, dividing the class into two teams and awarding a point for each correct suggestion.

Additional activity 2

Ask the class to brainstorm other types of shows; for example, puppet show, comedy, circus, pantomime, mime, church/classical music concert, light show, parade, laser show, fireworks. Now put students into pairs or threes and ask them to take it in turn to describe a kind of show, using language from Exercise 5. The others have to guess what kind of show it is.

Language focus

(Student's Book page 17)

Exercises 1 and 2

- Ask students to discuss the question in Exercise 1 briefly. They will find the answer in the text.

- Give students time to read the questions in Exercise 2. Tell them to look at the picture and scan the text very quickly to find the answers, and to call out as soon as they know them. Ask where they are likely to find the answer to the question in Exercise 1 (second paragraph). Ask students to read the second paragraph through quickly to find the answer.

Answers

1 Theatre began more than 2,500 years ago in Greece.

2 a first paragraph
  b second paragraph

Ask students to look at the pictures on page 16 and compare them with the picture of the amphitheatre. Students should talk about differences and similarities in groups.

Exercise 3

- Give students time to read the text in detail to find the answers to these questions. Then put them into pairs and ask them to talk about what they have found out, using their own words.

Exercises 4 and 5

- Students should recognize that question a is about the present, b is about the past, and c and d are about both. With the whole class, ask for sentences in answer to these questions, paying particular attention to the use of the verb forms. Encourage students to listen to and correct each other.

- Write the list of verbs on the board. Students should now be able to supply the past tense forms, referring to the text where necessary. They are all irregular except *danced* – ask how we know and remind them of the regular *-ed* ending for past tense verbs.

Answers					
a	began	c	danced	e	wore
b	sang	d	told		

Additional activity 4

Ask students to write *yes/no* questions about the text using the verbs in Exercise 5. Check their work, then put them into pairs and ask them to answer each other's questions. For example:

Did theatre begin in Rome?
– No, it didn't. It began in Greece.

This exercise revises the question and negative forms of the past simple.

Focus

- Put students into pairs and ask them to complete the exercises in the first section – remind them to use the negative where necessary!

Answers
do not/don't wear; is; act

- Give students time to look through the section dealing with the irregular past forms of these four verbs. Drill the words, to make sure students can pronounce them. Ask for example sentences using the verbs in both the present and past simple.

Additional activity 5

This activity expands the grammar in the Focus box. Write these sentences on the board and ask students to fill in the verbs. You can add your own sentences to these examples.

I was in England last year.
I ...... in England now. (Answer: *am*)

We didn't buy any cheese.
We never ...... cheese from the supermarket. (Answer: *buy*)

Did you bring your books to school?
...... your books to school every day? (Answer: *Do you bring*)

I don't catch a cold every winter.
I ...... a cold last winter. (Answer: *didn't catch*)

What does your teacher teach you?
What ...... your teacher ...... you yesterday? (Answer: *did*)

She usually goes swimming at the weekend.
She ...... swimming last weekend. (Answer: *went*)

Exercises 6 and 7 ❷

- Put students into pairs. Ask them to write the past forms they know and to guess the ones they are not sure of before looking at the list at the back of the book. Put pairs together into fours and ask them to compare their answers. Then play item 2 and ask them to check.

Answers			
1	was	7	had to
2	took	8	fell down
3	saw	9	began
4	was	10	looked
5	didn't/did not speak	11	didn't/did not have
6	forgot	12	enjoyed

TAPESCRIPT

It was my birthday last week, and my uncle and aunt took me to the theatre. I saw a play called *The Mission*. It was a really good story, but some of the cast didn't speak their lines very well. In fact, in the first half, an actor forgot his lines and another actor had to remind him.

In the second half of the play, part of the scenery fell down. The audience began to laugh and the actress on stage looked really angry. Altogether, the actors and actresses didn't have a very good evening. But I really enjoyed it!

Exercise 8

- In pairs or small groups, students describe a particular show, using the past simple tense. You could ask them to write this up as a paragraph for homework.

Additional activity 6

Ask students to write their own story in the past tense. They can write about what they did last night, last weekend, on their last holiday, etc. Make sure you check their writing.

Now ask them to rewrite their story – this time they leave out the past simple verbs and instead put the infinitives in brackets (as in Exercise 6). Ask them to exchange stories with a partner and to supply the past tense verbs in each other's stories. They can check their answers with their partner.

Additional activity 7

Make copies of photocopiable page 4 (one for each pair) and cut each list into separate slips. Put the class into pairs and tell them that the story starts with the sentence *Jim lived in a small house …* etc. Ask them to work together to assemble the other items into the right sequence of events to make a logical story. They should then discuss whether or not they think the story is true and exchange views with the rest of the class in discussion.

The correct sequence is: c, g, d, b, k, j, f, h, e, a, i

◯ Skills focus

(Student's Book page 18)

Exercise 1

- Put students into pairs and ask them to answer the questions. (As they will discover, the answer to the first one is rather tricky: although this looks like an old theatre, it is actually very new, being a modern reconstruction of Shakespeare's theatre, the Globe, in London.)

Exercise 2

- Keep students in their pairs for this exercise. They should take only a few seconds to find the answer to the first question (if they don't already know), but the second will take more careful sifting of the text. You could ask them to take notes under two headings: *Shakespeare's theatre* and *Theatres today*. Emphasize that we are comparing past and present here, so students should pay close attention to the verb forms they use.

Answers

a William Shakespeare

b *Possible answer:* In Shakespeare's theatre there was no scenery, there were no actresses on stage and most of the audience stood up. Today there is scenery, there are actresses on stage and the audience sits in seats.

- You might like to point out that the dates indicate when Shakespeare was born and died. Ask students how to say them (1564 = fifteen sixty-four, 1616 = sixteen sixteen.) Check that students know how to ask these two questions: *When was Shakespeare born? When did Shakespeare die?*

Exercise 3

- Ask students to write down their questions. Monitor carefully and help with questions and vocabulary. Then put the students into pairs and ask them to ask and answer each other's questions.

Additional activity 8

Ask students to do a project on Shakespeare and find out as much information as they can. Students then put their information on to posters which you can display around the classroom. Bring in any extra material that you can find. You may like to divide your class into groups and give each one a topic to research and write about. Possible topics:

William Shakespeare's life
Life in 16th century England
The Globe Theatre
The works of Shakespeare – his most famous plays
The storyline of a Shakespeare play

Exercise 4 🔲 ❸

- Tell students that Emma is giving a presentation about Eastern theatre. Ask the class to brainstorm questions about what they expect to find out about this topic. They will then listen to discover what Emma asks and finds out.

- Play item 3 and ask students to write down Emma's three questions. Check these with the whole class, writing the questions on the board. Then replay the tape and ask students to make notes on the answers to the questions. They should compare notes in pairs, then listen once again to check their answers.

 TAPESCRIPT

Hi everybody! I'm Emma, and today I'm going to talk to you about Eastern theatre. But before I start, let's see how much you know about Western theatre today. Can you answer these three easy questions? Number 1: Do actors usually wear masks? Number 2: Do they wear make-up? Number 3: Is there always some scenery on stage?

Exercise 5

- In pairs, students study the table (helping each other with vocabulary if necessary) and look at the picture to see what information they can fill in.

Exercises 6 and 7 ❹

- Play item 4 and ask students to check their answers and make short notes. Pause the tape where necessary to allow them time to write. Ask students to discuss their answers in pairs.

Suggested answers

wigs: none

scenery: very simple

actors: all men

actresses: none

movements: everything done through movements; all have exact meaning

words: none

music: in background all through play

- Ask students to say what other details they remember. Play item 4 again and ask students to expand their notes and add more details. Play the tape once again if necessary. Go through the answers with the whole class.

 TAPESCRIPT

Well done! All your answers were correct of course. But Eastern theatre is very different from Western theatre nowadays. Especially the Noh theatre of Japan.

Noh theatre began 600 years ago, in the 14th century. All the actors wear wooden masks. There are gods, ghosts, ladies and all sorts of different characters in the stories and they all wear different masks. This is how you know who they are. The actors don't wear costumes or wigs.

There are no actresses, only actors – in other words, only men. An actor begins to learn the rules of Noh Theatre at the age of seven. Everything is done through movements. There are no words. Each movement he makes has an exact meaning, for example, a Noh actor never cries on stage the way a person does in real life. He holds a hand under his eyes and bows his head. He doesn't make any noise. But the audience understands that he is crying.

The scenery is very simple, and there is music in the background all the way through the play.

Exercise 8

- Put students into pairs and ask them to use their notes to write about Noh Theatre. Then put two pairs with each other and ask pairs to take turns in reading their texts out loud. As they listen, they should suggest a correction for anything they think is a mistake.

Exercise 9

- In groups, students research theatre traditions in your country. Ask them to find out as much as they can and make notes, using library resources and any material you may be able to supply. Each group should then work out how they can present the information to the rest of the class, making sure that every member of the group contributes in some way.

- Ask students to write individual reports on the information gathered by their group. This could be set as a homework exercise,

⬤ Dancing in the Street

Exercises 1, 2 and 3 🔲 ❺

- Use the picture to set the scene and mood for the song.

- Ask students to read the list of places and say where they are. Can anyone recognize or guess what the USSR was? If not, let them know what the letters stand for (Union of Soviet Socialist Republics) and see if anyone can work out the answer. Some students may also know that *Back in the USSR* is the name of a Beatles song.

- Play the tape and ask students to fill in the blanks. When they sing along, they can substitute names of places in their own country.

TAPESCRIPT

Calling out, around the world
Are you ready for a brand new beat?
Summer's here and the time is right
For dancing in the street
Dancing in Chicago
Down in New Orleans

In New York City
All we need is music
Sweet music, there'll be music everywhere
There'll be swinging, swaying, records playing
Dancing in the street

It doesn't matter what you wear
Just as long as you are there
So, come on, every guy, grab a girl
Everywhere, around the world
There'll be dancing
Dancing in the street
There'll be dancing
Dancing in the street …

Think about it!

These exercises are a basic round-up of the language taught in the unit. They can be done individually or in pairs in class, or for homework, then checked in the next lesson.

Answers

1 1 scenery   2 orchestra   3 actress   4 ballet
   5 lights
2 wore; catch; bought; taught
3 Students' own answers
4 Students' own answers

Workbook answers

1
1 stage 2 audience 3 seats 4 actor 5 orchestra
6 scenery 7 wings

2
1 1066 2 1594 3 1999 4 520 5 1616
6 1845 7 1224

3 (Suggested answers)
The director is shouting / holding the script.
The children are singing.
The woman is sewing/mending a costume.
The men are carrying a ladder.
The man is hanging from the curtain.
The boy is falling off the stage.
The baby is crying.
The dog is barking / attacking the director.
A fire is burning.

4
1 took 2 began 3 spoke 4 forgot 5 bought
6 brought

5
2 Did you come by train?
3 Did she teach Science?
4 When did you go to bed?
6 No, he took me to the cinema.
7 No, I cooked a pizza.
8 They were in Australia/Sydney last summer.

6
1 lives	5 started	9 love	13 watches
2 went	6 enjoys	10 takes	14 takes
3 wanted	7 was	11 doesn't work	15 came
4 does	8 got	12 stopped	16 hope

7
2 No, he wasn't.   5 No, he hasn't.
3 Yes. he does.   6 Yes, they do.
4 Yes, she is.   7 No, they/it didn't.

8
2 Why did Uncle Bob leave / go away from Scotland?
3 When did Uncle Bob start playing baseball?
4 When did Uncle Bob get married?
5 What does Aunt Julia do?
6 When did Uncle Bob stop working?
7 How often does Aunt Julia take pictures?

9 Students' own answers
Flick back!
• shout, sing
• easy
• began, told, stood
• wooden

Buzz words

fell, did, sang, wore, bought, took, saw, spoke, forgot, made, went, had, came, began, was

Heroes and villains

Learning objectives

- describing people
- telling stories
- describing events/actions

Language focus

- revision of tenses
- past simple for narratives
- adverbs

Active vocabulary

attractive	diamond	friendly
gun	hero	intelligent
island	slim	taxi
unattractive	unfriendly	unintelligent
villain		

Receptive vocabulary

adverb	air	airport
appearance	breakfast	calmly
carefully	check in	cold
driver	event	excitedly
heart-shaped	high	hot
immediately	in the middle of	nervously
novel (*noun*)	personality	politely
recognize	search	sky
suddenly	suit (*noun*)	surprised
swamp	terrace	until
worriedly		

Lead-ins

a To revise the past simple tense and practise telling stories in the past, ask pairs to re-tell the story of 'The theatre tickets' (photocopiable page 4) in their own words.

b Ask students to rank themselves from the oldest to the youngest. They could sit in order of age for this lesson. Students tell each other when they were born and then stand in the correct place.

c Write two columns on the board – *Heroes* and *Villains*. Ask students to brainstorm the names of heroes and villains. Then ask them to think of adjectives that can be used to describe both types of people.

d Write the title *In Search of the Blue Diamond* on the board. Put these words underneath:

*nervously   sister   diamond   map   airport   run
heart-shaped rock   new friend   fat man*

Put students in groups and ask them to use the title and words to guess what the story is about.

Materials

Copies of photocopiable activity, Unit 4 for Lead-in a.

Copies of photocopiable page 5 for Additional activity 4.

Sellotape or pins for Additional activity 9.

Vocabulary
(Student's Book page 20)

Exercise 1

- Do Lead-in c to get students thinking about the topic. This will also familiarize them with words that they might need to use in Exercise 3. Write students' suggestions on the board and use this lead-in as a way of pre-teaching *ambitious, hard-working, tough, adventurous, mean, glamorous, dangerous*. Write the words on the board.

- Put students into groups and ask them to sort the adjectives into the two categories.

Answers

a slim, attractive, fat, short, tall

b unfriendly, intelligent, unintelligent, friendly, unattractive

- Ask the class to sort the ten adjectives into pairs of opposites.

Exercise 2

- Students look at the words on the board from Lead-in c and classify them as either a or b. Then ask them to think of two or three more adjectives that belong in each group. Encourage them to help each other, to use dictionaries or to ask you for an L1 translation if necessary.

- If you think your students can manage, ask them to find opposites for their adjectives.

Additional activity 1

Tell students to jot down three animals – the first three that come to mind – and then an adjective to describe each one. They should do this quickly, without thinking hard about it; if they like, they can write first in L1 and then get a translation. They might write something like: *sweet rabbit, mean tiger, happy cat.*

Now tell students that they can analyse their own personalities! Their first adjective + animal shows how other people see them; the second one is how they view themselves and the third shows what they would like to be. In groups, students can look at each other's words and discuss how appropriate the 'analysis' is. (This is of course just a game, not a real psychological test!)

Exercise 3

- Divide the class into three, six or nine groups (a multiple of three) and name them A, B or C. Ask the A group(s) to look at the picture of Amanda and describe her as fully as possibly, using the expressions in the exercise. Bs do the same for Micky and Cs for the two villains, Maxwell and Tara. Help students with vocabulary and language.

- When students are ready, make up new groups of three, containing a student from A, one from B and one from C. Students take it in turn to describe their picture to the others.

- Put the names of the three characters on the board and gather as many suggestions as possible from the whole class for the three types of sentence.

Exercise 4

- Students discuss the question in pairs or threes. Help students by giving them this example: *My father looks mean and angry but he isn't. He's very kind and calm.*

- We use *He/She is …* when we know this for a fact. We can either see that the description is true (*She's tall, He's old*, etc.) or we know the person and are giving a firm opinion (*She's very talkative, He's intelligent*). If we don't know the person and are judging by appearances, then we use *He/She looks … She looks intelligent* (we don't know this – maybe it's because she's wearing glasses); *He looks sad* (but maybe he always looks like this!)

Exercise 5

- Ask students to describe film, TV or book characters. Build up notes on the board, making a clear distinction between *He/She is …* and *He/She looks …*

Additional activity 2

Put students into large groups and ask them to take it in turns to describe a teacher in the school. The others in the group have to guess who it is.

Additional activity 3

Ask students to describe themselves (appearance and personality). They should write five descriptive sentences which are true and two which are false. In small groups, students take it in turns to read out their descriptions, and the others try to find the false information.

discuss the answers in their groups, and then check with the whole class. When discussing c, make sure students understand that Carrie is being held prisoner by the man on the phone.

Answers

a Amanda is a writer/novelist or Amanda writes novels.

b Carrie

c No – she is the man's prisoner ('We've got your sister') and she is obviously very scared ('You have to help me')

d He wants the Blue Diamond.

Additional activity 5

Put students into groups of three and ask them to take one role each: Amanda, Carrie and the man on the phone. Ask them to re-read the text and mark the characters' names next to the things they say. They should then rehearse the scene. Encourage them to bring out the feelings of the characters – point out the words *nervously*, *worriedly* and *calmly*. Choose some groups to act out their scene in front of the class.

Exercise 3

• Ask students to do this exercise individually, and then check answers with the whole class.

Answers

a stopped, picked up, asked,

b was, heard, said

c you'll never see

d We're going to keep

e is that you?, You have to help, Where are you? you bring, I don't know, We want

f What's happening?, what you're talking about

Additional activity 6

If you feel that students need revision of tenses, ask pairs to add two or three more examples of their own to categories a–f.

If you want to revise the past simple, write three columns on the board and ask students to add more verbs from the text. For example:

Base form	Past simple	Regular/irregular?
ring	rang	irregular
stop	stopped	regular

Additional activity 4

Pairwork: make enough copies of photocopiable page 5 for each pair, and cut them into A and B parts. Students help each other to fill the gaps. The completed story will give them more insight into the personality and life-style of Micky Curtis. It also makes a link with the film *In Search of the Blue Diamond*, which forms the basis for the rest of the unit. The complete version of the story is as follows:

Villain or hero?

Micky Curtis was a very famous, rich film star. He was very attractive and acted beautifully. He always played the hero's part in his films, which made a lot of money.

There was one big problem, however. He did not make friends easily because he was so difficult to work with. He told film directors what they should do. He shouted angrily at the other actors and told them that they were not good enough to work with him.

Micky only talked happily about one thing: himself. He talked about his money, his big houses, fast cars and private planes. He often said he was the best actor in the world.

One afternoon, they were filming a scene for the film *In Search of the Blue Diamond*. A young camerawoman asked Micky politely to move. She needed to get past him with her camera. Micky looked at her angrily and started shouting loudly.

'Do you know who you are talking to? I'm Micky Curtis, the hero of show business. My films always sell successfully. I'm the best actor and the richest man in the world. I've got millions of dollars in the bank. What have you got?'

The camerawoman looked at Micky thoughtfully. Then she answered happily, 'I've got friends!'

Language focus
(Student's Book page 21)

Exercise 1

• Do Lead-in d to arouse students' interest in the story and help them predict what it is about. Then put them into groups and ask them to talk about the picture. With the whole class, elicit suggestions about what is happening.

Exercise 2

• Students now look at the comprehension questions a–d and read the text. Ask them to

Focus

- Students should recognize that the main tense in the story is the simple past. However, point out that we use other tenses (present tenses, in this case) when we write the exact words that people say.

- Remind students of the phrase *Amanda said nervously*, and elicit the point that adverbs go with verbs – their function is to describe how the person does the action. Ask students to underline all the adverbs in the text (*nervously, worriedly, carefully, calmly*.) and make sure they notice the *-ly* ending. Here are some other guidelines that they may find helpful.

  1 Adverbs are formed by adding *-ly* to the adjective:
  nervous – nervously; careful – carefully

  2 Adjectives that end in *-y* drop the *-y* and add *-ily* to make the adverb:
  happy – happily; busy – busily

  3 The adverb form of *good* is *well*.

  4 The following are both adjectives and adverbs:
  late fast hard early

Additional activity 7

Ask students to prepare two separate pieces of paper. On one piece, they should write down an adverb. Encourage them to think of others apart from those they have already met. On the other piece of paper, they should write down an activity. Encourage students to be creative! For example: washing an elephant, eating spaghetti, etc. Put students into large groups (or do this as a whole class if numbers allow) and ask them to put their adverb papers in one pile (face down) and the activities in another pile. Students take it in turns to pick a slip from each pile. They must then mime the activity in the manner of the adverb. The others have to guess what the activity and adverb are.

Exercise 4

- Put students into groups and ask them to use the pictures to guess what is going to happen next in the story. Asks students to make notes of their ideas. Then tell students to walk around the class, asking and telling each other about their ideas.

Skills focus

(Student's Book page 22)

Exercise 1

- Ask students to scan the text quickly to find the answers to the questions.

Answers
a Moronia
b Cartawaya (late in the evening) Devil's Island (early afternoon)

Exercise 2

- Ask students to find the answers to the questions and then discuss their ideas in twos or threes. Ask them to say how they came to their conclusions. This exercise encourages students to 'read between the lines' and infer meaning – an important skill when reading or listening.

Answers
a a gun
b The young man had knocked him down.

Exercise 3

- Put students into pairs for Exercise 3. Ask them to start by writing down what they think these irregular past tenses might be. They then check in the passage, writing the correct line numbers in the boxes.

Answers		
drank 29	went 21, 23	put 1
felt 32	had to 48	saw 3, 7, 45
got 13	heard 32	stood 34
gave 14	knew 5, 9	took 29, 42

Additional activity 8

Play 'Bingo'. Ask students to draw a rectangle with twelve squares in it and to write in the past simple form of six verbs. Students can choose from the verbs in Exercise 3 and about ten others which you should write up on the board. Make sure that you write the infinitive of the verb on the board, but that students write the past form. Now call out the verbs in the infinitive, in any order, and ask students to cross out the corresponding past simple forms if they have them. When a student has crossed out all six squares, he/she calls out 'Bingo!' Check that the student's answers are correct.

(Note that you can also play 'Bingo' to revise opposites or synonyms of vocabulary to be found in the book.)

Exercise 4

- In pairs or small groups, students order the events – these come from the text as a whole, starting from Part 1 on page 21.

Answer

Correct order: d, f, c, a, e, b

- Ask students to notice the tense that is used for these questions and draw their attention to the 'Look!' box on page 23. Explain that when you write a story or talk about what you did in the past, you use the past simple. However, if you are telling someone about the story of a book, film, play etc., or if you are telling a joke, you normally use the present simple.

Exercise 5

- Ask students to write a paragraph about the main events of the story, using the present simple as in Exercise 4. Put them in pairs to compare paragraphs. Alternatively, you could ask them to use their paragraphs to summarize the story in a chain around the class: the first student starts with something like *First, Amanda gets a phone call,* then the second adds a sentence, and so on around the class.

Additional activity 8

Ask students to pick out the two adverbs in the second-last paragraph of the text and to say what verbs they go with. What do they tell us about Amanda's actions?

Ask each student to write an adverb on a piece of paper and stick it on to someone else's back, making sure that the other person cannot see what the adverb is. Ask the class to suggest a simple sentence (or choose one from the text) – the content is not important. The aim of the activity is for students to guess what adverb they have stuck to their backs. They walk around the class asking classmates to say the sentence in the manner of that adverb, and then try to guess what it is from the way their partner reads/behaves. If they cannot guess the adverb immediately, they move on to find someone else to help them.

Exercise 6

- In small groups, students discuss what will happen next. Will Amanda get the Blue Diamond? Will she save her sister? Point out the difference between *So do I* and *Neither do I*.

- Ask each group to tell the whole class how they think the story will end.

Exercise 9

- Ask students to sit back and listen to the end of the story. Remind them that the Reading tip is also true for listening – as long as they can understand the main idea and follow the story, they should not worry about every word they do not know. Play item 1 once or twice and then ask students to tell each other what happens. This will help them with comprehension and give them practise in talking about a story in the present tenses.

- Ask groups to compare the ending with their ideas. Are they similar? Which ending do they think is best – the one on the tape or their own?

TAPESCRIPT

She turned to her new friend.

'Are you coming with me, or not?'

'I don't think so,' the young man calmly replied. He had the gun and he was pointing it at Amanda. Behind him were the fat man and the woman from the hotel. 'I told you it would work,' said the young man. He laughed wickedly. He turned to Amanda. 'We don't need you any more,' he said. 'But what about my sister? She's in danger … I have to help her.' The young man pointed his gun at Amanda and fired.

Suddenly Amanda woke up. Her heart was racing. She felt very frightened. She looked nervously around the room. 'Where am I?' she thought. Then she realized. It was her bedroom, it was 7 a.m., and she was in bed. It was all just a bad dream, a very bad dream. 'But it felt so real,' she thought as she slowly got out of bed. She made herself a cup of strong black coffee. The old map and the pages of her novel were still on her desk. Amanda smiled to herself. 'I've just got too much imagination'.

She sat down and started to type a new page. The telephone rang. Amanda stopped typing her novel and picked up the phone.

'Hello?'

'Amanda?'

'Carrie, is that you?' asked Amanda worriedly.

'Yes, help me! You have to help me …'

Untitled

Think about it!

These exercises are a basic round-up of the language taught in the unit. They can be done individually or in pairs in class, or for homework, then checked in the next lesson.

Answers

1 1 intelligent   2 tall, short   3 unfriendly
   4 attractive

2 1 walked   2 had   3 checked   4 went
   5 got   6 heard   7 turned   8 saw
   9 shouted   10 pointed   11 said

Workbook answers

1 (Suggested answers)

1 She's tall and slim. She's got short hair. She looks attractive/intelligent.

2 He's short and fat. He's got big eyes and big ears / short hair. He looks friendly/funny.

3 He's tall and fat. He's got long hair. He looks unfriendly/unattractive.

2

3 isn't sharp enough.   5 run fast enough.
4 early enough.   6 is too heavy.

3

1 faster   4 cheapest   7 heavier
2 fastest   5 older   8 lightest
3 cheaper   6 oldest   9 heaviest

4

b 2 c 9 d 7 e 6 f 4 g 3 h 1 i 5

5

b He had breakfast.
c He rang his friend Peter.
d He left the house.
e He stood in the rain.
f He caught the number 9 bus.
g He went to his friend's house.
h They sat on the beach.
i They drank coffee.
j He came home.
k He ate dinner.
l He went to bed at 11 o'clock.

6

a T b F c T d T e F f F

7 Students' own answers

Flick back!

- library card: Unit 1
- alien's song: Unit 3
- town map: Unit 4, Revision Units 1–5
- questionnaire: Unit 6
- school report: Unit 14
- boiling oil: Unit 13
- quiz: Unit 16
- recipe: Unit 17

Buzz words

Across: 2 went   4 bought   6 gave   7 sang
   8 caught   10 flew   11 made   13 felt   15 took
   16 had   17 sat   18 knew

Down: 1 stood   2 wore   3 rang   5 heard   6 got
   8 came   9 slept   10 felt   12 drank   14 sold
   17 saw

Revision

Units 1–5

Stop and think!

The exercises and activities in this unit revise all the language taught in Units 1–5. It is divided into five sections A–E. The HELP screen suggests extra help or activities. Encourage students to refer to these while they are working or set them as homework. When they can do each section, students can colour the letters.

A Question words

(Student's Book page 24)

Exercise 1

- Look at the picture with students and elicit the point that Tom went to a football match.
- Get students to say what words questions can begin with and write their suggestions on the board, e.g. *Where/When/Who/What/How*, etc.
- Ask students to read the whole dialogue and then fill in the gaps with the correct question word. They should read the dialogue aloud with a partner taking it in turns to ask and answer.

Answers				
Where	Who	How far	How	How long
Did	What	Are	Will	Has	Can

Exercise 2

- In pairs, students ask each other questions about what they did last weekend. Go around and monitor, correcting question forms where necessary. Tell students to make notes and choose a few to report back to the class.

B Food

(Student's Book page 25)

Exercise 1

- Let students look at the picture of different items of food for a few minutes. Ask a few questions to check understanding. *How much is a lettuce? How much are potatoes?* Point out that *per* is not the usual spoken word – we usually say *a*, e.g. *35p a kilo* and this is an unstressed syllable.
- In pairs or small groups, students complete the questions and work out the answers. Get the whole class to report back and write up the answers on the board.

Answers		
1	35p	4 How much; £2.10
2	How many; 18	5 How many; 3
3	How much; £2.50	6 How much; half a kilo

Exercise 2

- Do this exercise with the whole class, starting off by copying the diagram for curry on the board and eliciting the other ingredients. Different students can take your place at the board for the other four dishes, making similar diagrams from the class's suggestions.
- Remind students of the passive constructions *is/are made with*, *filled with* and *served with*. Students work individually to make sentences about a dish they know, without mentioning its name. Pairs then read each other's sentences and try to guess the dish. Encourage them to help each other to correct any grammatical or spelling errors.

C *going to*

(Student's Book page 25)

Exercise 1

- Ask students to talk about the pictures on page 97 with a partner. They should say what the person or animal is going to do, using the prompts to make complete sentences. Ask the whole class to repeat the correct sentences.

Answers
1 He's going to set fire to the house.
2 The dogs are going to attack him. (b)
3 She's not going to dive into the pool. (c)
4 They're not going to sunbathe today. (e)
5 He's going to break the glass. (a)

Exercise 2

- Tell students that Sara is going to California. Allow class discussion about what they know about it and what they think it is like. Elicit some of the students' own questions to ask Sara about her holiday plans without looking at the questions in the exercise. Go through the example prompt *you/stay/big hotel* and drill the question form *Are you going to stay in a big hotel?* Ask students to make the questions for prompts 1–5.

- In pairs, they ask and answer the questions, then write in the questions and answers.

Answers

1 Are you going to visit Hollywood?
2 Is your sister going to travel with you?
3 Are you going to swim in the Pacific?
4 Are you going to look for film stars?
5 Are you going to go surfing?

D Adverbs

(Student's Book page 26)

Exercise 1

- Copy the incomplete table of adjectives and adverbs on to the board and ask students to come up and fill in the gaps. Ask for suggestions to add to the table, e.g. *quiet/quietly*, *happy/happily*, *excited/excitedly*, etc.

Answers

slow – slowly   worried – worriedly
calm – calmly   careful – carefully
polite – politely   nervous – nervously
immediate – immediately

Exercise 2

- Ask students to read the sentences 1–6 and choose a suitable adverb from the table in Exercise 1.

Answers

1 worriedly   3 suddenly   5 immediately
2 calmly   4 politely   6 carefully

E Irregular verbs

(Student's Book page 26)

Exercise 1

- Focus students' attention on the picture of a family picnic. Ask if they enjoy picnics. If anyone has any stories about a picnic, let them tell the rest of the class. Tell students to read the passage and put the verbs in brackets into the past simple. You may like them to do this as a test or as homework. Go through the answers by asking different students to read a sentence each. Explain any vocabulary they are not sure of but encourage them to guess unknown words.

Answers

1 went 2 forgot 3 had to 4 took 5 stopped
6 began 7 sat 8 drank 9 made
10 burned/burnt 11 stood 12 ran 13 told
14 got 15 was 16 put 17 said 18 heard
19 saw 20 knew 21 gave 22 brought

Reading and writing

(Student's Book page 27)

Exercise 1

- With closed books, ask students some general knowledge questions about Australia: *How long does it take to get there (from their country)? What is the capital city? Can you name any Australian animals? What language do people speak?* etc. Turn to Exercise 1 on page 27 and ask students to read Ralph's letter from Australia and put each sentence below it into the correct paragraph.

Answers

1 B 2 E 3 D 4 A 5 C

Exercise 2

- Ask students to think of a place they would like to visit or a place they have been to already and to imagine they are on holiday there. Get them to write notes using the prompts given.

Exercise 3

- Students use their notes to write a letter. This can be done in class or as homework.

Project idea

(Student's Book page 27)

Talk about the picture on page 27 with the whole class. As homework, ask students to cut out as many pictures from magazines and newspapers as they can find and make a collage picture. The skyscraper sandwich can be of anything they like. Set a time for them to bring in their pictures and talk about them. Put them on the walls and let the class choose the best ones.

Join the club!

Learning objectives

- talking about interests
- talking about hobbies
- saying what the requirements are for different clubs and societies
- reading a letter for information

Language focus

- verb + gerund (*I am interested in ..., I don't like ...*)
- *need to/have to/needn't/don't have to*

Active vocabulary

aerobics	badge	chess
club	coin	collect
have to	hobby	horse-riding
instrument	jewellery	join
model (*noun*)	need to	practise
stamp (*noun*)		

Receptive vocabulary

birthday	birthday present	brush (*noun*)
cassette	CD	cotton (*adjective*)
cycling	display (*verb*)	exercise
fabric paint	fee	fill in
fit (*adjective*)	folk dancing	form (*noun*)
Geology	gymnastics	ice-skating
necessary	painting	penfriend
polish (*verb*)	poster	shelf
society	stone	

Materials

Prospectuses from universities, colleges, or English language schools (in Britain) which describe different clubs and societies for Vocabulary Exercise 1 and Language Focus Exercise 1.

Information about genuine penfriends clubs for Skills Focus Exercise 1.

A letter from another country for Skills Focus Exercise 1.

Pictures from magazines or newspapers of different hobbies (e.g. cookery, pottery, sports, collections), mounted on card if possible, for Lead-in a and Additional activity 1.

Copies of photocopiable page 6 for Additional activity 6.

Lead-ins

a Before the lesson, attach to the board any pictures you have collected of hobbies or sports. Try to include something you enjoy yourself! Introduce yourself, giving your name, and then say a little bit about your own hobbies and interests, pointing to the appropriate picture(s) as you do so. Give vocabulary for the pictures you have collected.

Ask a student *What's your name?* and *What are you interested in?* using the pictures on the board as prompts if necessary. Do the same with different students.

Students work in pairs, finding out as much as they can about their partner, including their hobbies (you can give word prompts on the board, e.g. name, age, nationality, hobbies). They feed back about their partner in the third person to the class, giving their name, age and interests. Encourage students to use *interested in* or *don't like* + noun or gerund, but do not make this a teaching point yet as the emphasis should be on encouraging everyone to speak. Check comprehension by asking students questions, e.g. *What is Christos interested in?*

b Write *interested* on the board. Tell students that they have two minutes to write as many words as they can think of using the letters in the word on the board. For example: *in, enter, rest, test,* etc.

Vocabulary

(Student's Book page 28)

Exercise 1

- Most British schools, colleges and language schools have societies and clubs you can join in addition to academic courses. If possible, show students some brochures or prospectuses, pointing out the different activities on offer. Explain that sometimes there are certain requirements for joining a club. For example, if you want to learn aerobics you need to be in good health, if you want to learn tennis you need a tennis racket.

- Ask students to open their books. Read question a aloud. Give students a few minutes to study the poster and discuss with their partners what they think it is advertising.

- Look at the poster as a class, eliciting as much vocabulary as you can (allow students to tell you what they know). Drill any new words.

- Pick individual students and ask them to give you the names of different activities you point out, using your own pictures or the poster in the Student's Book.

> #### Additional activity 1
>
> Divide the class into two teams, A and B. Draw a noughts and crosses chart on the board.
>
> Using your own pictures of school club activities or those on the poster in the Student's Book, ask teams one at a time to give you the word for a club or activity you point out. If they get it correct, they can come and put a nought or cross on the chart. If not, the question goes to the other team. If neither team gets it correct, give them the word, drill it, and come back to it later.

Exercise 2

- Ask the students to look at the words in the box on page 28. They should match the verbs on the left with the corresponding nouns on the right to list the activities you can do in clubs or societies. Do the first one with them.

- Ask them if they can think of any more activities to add to the list.

Exercise 3

- Ask students if they have any clubs or societies at school and if any of them are members.

- Ask students to look at the poster in Exercise 1 again and decide which of those clubs or societies they would like to join. Give them time to discuss and decide. Remind them to use phrases like I'd like to join/I wouldn't like to join … because …, I'm interested in … because …

- Go over their answers with the class, asking them why they made their choices.

Exercise 4

- Students work in pairs, asking about any other activities and hobbies they are interested in, and which they don't like.

- Ask a few students to feed back their sentences to the class. Make sure students are using the structures from Exercise 3 (interested in and don't like).

> #### Additional activity 2
>
> Pick four to six students (depending on class size). Ask them to come to the front and write down two sentences about each group member on a piece of paper, the first sentence using enjoy, and the second using interested in. Collect them in and attach them to the board so the class can see them.
>
> Play a guessing game. One of the students at the front stands up, and the class has to guess which are his/her hobbies, by choosing two sentences from the ones on the board. (Students have to put their hands up if they think they know the answers.) For example: He is interested in chess. He enjoys football. If they are right, the student sits down. If not, they try to guess the next person's hobbies.

Language focus

(Student's Book page 29)

Exercise 1

- Explain that the word society means a club or group which you can join if you are interested in the activity it offers.

- Show students some of the prospectuses you have brought in if you have them. Remind them that for some activities there are certain requirements.

- If you have a prospectus, point out an activity, such as swimming, and say clearly: You need a swimming costume. You need to be able to swim. If you do not have a prospectus, use the picture in the book of the music society and make a sentence about this: You need to enjoy music.

- Focus on the photo on page 29. Ask the students to tell you as much as they can about it, for example, *Where is it? What kind of society do you think it is? What can you see on the table?*

▶ **Note**

For obligation, *need to* or *have to* can be used:

Affirmative: *you need* + infinitive of verb, for example, *You need to fill in this form, You need to be able to play an instrument.*

have to + infinitive of verb, for example, *You have to sing a song.*

When there is no obligation *don't have to* can be used, for example, *You don't have to pay a fee.*

- Read the instructions, and remind students to look at the picture. Students take a few minutes to write their answers to the questions. Check with the class by asking individual students to offer you their answers.

Answers

Students can offer alternative answers for all the questions apart from a, as long as they are correct in the context.

a   It is a music society.

b   You can learn to play instruments, you can learn to sing, you can join an orchestra or choir and you can listen to music.

c   He may be asking for more information about the club. He may be asking which instruments you can learn. He may be asking if he needs to play an instrument or read music to join.

Exercise 2 📼 ❶

- Play item 1, asking students to check their answers to Exercise 1.

- Play the cassette a second time if necessary, pausing at the relevant points on the dialogue.

📼 TAPESCRIPT

Girl   Hello. Can I help you?

Boy   Yes, I was wondering … erm … what do I have to do to become a member of the Music Society?

Girl   Well, first you need to fill in this form, saying what kind of music you like, what instrument you play, what …

Boy   Instrument? Do I have to be able to play an instrument?

Girl   No, you don't have to but it's more interesting if you do. Do you like music, at least?

Boy   Oh yeah, I love it. Erm … do I need to pay a fee to join?

Girl   No, of course not. It's free. Oh, by the way, have you got any CDs or cassettes?

Boy   Yes, I've got quite a few. Why? Do I have to bring them?

Girl   No, you don't have to, but sometimes we like to listen to different kinds of music in our meetings.

Boy   Oh good, I've got some great CDs. Er … is there anything else I need to know?

Girl   Yes, there is something … You have to sing a song in your first meeting.

Boy   Sing a song?

Girl   Yes, all our new members have to do it.

Boy   What if I can't sing very well?

Girl   Well, we just won't ask you to join the choir, then!

Exercise 3

- Students look at the list in their books (page 29). Ask them if they can remember any of the dialogue from Exercise 2 and see if they can tick any of the boxes.

- Tell them to listen to the dialogue again and tick the boxes for the things the boy *has to/needs to* or *doesn't have to do*. Then play the cassette.

- Check the answers with the class.

Answers

have to/need to: fill in a form, sing a song

don't have to: be able to play an instrument, pay a fee, bring CDs or cassettes

Additional activity 3

In pairs, ask students to role-play the conversation between the boy and girl, referring to the answers in Exercise 3. Allow willing pairs to come to the front and act out their role-play to the class.

Focus

- Read through the explanation of *need to/have to/don't have to*. Point out that *need to* and *have to* in the affirmative mean *must* (it is obligatory), but *don't have to* in the negative means *you can, but it is not essential* (it is distinct from *mustn't* which means *it is prohibited*).

- Give students a few minutes to look at the example sentences in the box, and then ask them questions a, b and c.

- Once you are certain they understand the differences between the verbs, ask them to complete the sentences: We can use *need to* or *have to* for things which are necessary. We can use *don't have to* for things which aren't necessary.

- Then ask students to look at their completed list in Exercise 3 again. In pairs, they talk about what is or isn't necessary for joining the music society. Do an example with the class if necessary.

Additional activity 4

In pairs or groups, students think of their own club or society, but do not tell the class what it is. They then take it in turns to give sentences about the society, using *need to*/*have to* or *don't have to*. The other students must try to guess what the society is from the sentences.

Exercise 4

- Students work in pairs or groups and choose a hobby. Ask individuals, *What is your hobby?* to check comprehension.

- They then make a chart (like the one shown) of things you have to/need to do or don't have to do to do the hobby.

- Students then tell the rest of the class about their hobby and what is or isn't necessary to do it. Let the rest of the class guess what the hobby is.

Skills focus

(Student's Book page 30)

Exercise 1

- Check students understand what a penfriend is. If possible, show the students a letter you have from a friend in Britain or another country. Explain that you can be friends with someone you have never met by writing letters to them. Usually penfriends live in another part of the world, and provide an opportunity to learn about other cultures and ways of life. You might like to explain that the word comes from linking the word *pen* with the word *friend*, because we write to penfriends but don't talk to them and rarely meet them.

- If you have any real information about a penfriends club, show it to the students, explaining that they might like to consider joining it. (They should check with their parents first.) If not, explain that there is a society or club you can join if you want a penfriend. The club will put you in touch with students in other countries who also want a penfriend.

- Ask if anyone in the class has a penfriend. Students might like to talk a bit about their penfriends. Give them a minute to do this.

- Ask what kind of things you might write about in a letter to someone you have never met. What kind of things could you tell someone in England (for example) about your country?

- Read out the introduction in Exercise 1. Focus on the photos on page 30 and see if students can guess what the letters are going to be about.

- Give any additional vocabulary the students may ask for, e.g. *stones, quartz, fossils, frame, dye.*

Exercise 2

- Divide the class into pairs or groups of As and Bs.

- Explain that Student A must only look at letter A and Student B must only look at letter B. Ask them to cover the other letter with a book or paper.

- Go over the headings in the table on page 30, ensuring the students understand them, and explain that they only need to make notes in each column. Give an example *(hobby: football, when started: 1995)*.

- a: Go round checking students have matched their letter with the correct picture and are confident about making notes in the table in the correct column. Give students three minutes to make their notes.

- b: In pairs or groups, Student As first tell Student Bs about their letter and Student Bs fill in the information in their blank column A.

- Remind students to refer to their notes but to use full sentences while they are speaking, for example, *His hobby is collecting stones.* Go round checking the students' sentences.

- c: Students swap over and Bs tell As about their letter. Check by asking A students to put their hands up. Ask one at a time to tell you something about B's letter. Ask Bs to say if they are right or wrong.

- Swap over and ask Bs to tell you something about A's letter and As to say if they are right or wrong.

- d: Tell the students they can now read the other letter and check their own notes.

Look!

- Read out the sentence given as an example: *You needn't spend a lot of money.*

- Explain the meaning of *needn't*: when something is not necessary. (Remind students of the Language focus point on *don't have to*.)

Exercise 3

- a: Go through the headings in the table in Exercise 2 again. Check that students understand them.
- Give students a few minutes to write notes about their hobby, for example, *when started: 1995.*
- b: Look at the paragraph plan with students and check they understand how they should use their notes for each paragraph. Then give them time to write the three paragraphs about their hobbies.
- c: Divide the class into pairs or groups and ask them to read each other's letters.
- The class can then vote to decide which hobby they think is the most interesting.

Additional activity 5

Students find someone in the class who has the same hobby as they do, by moving around and asking questions. When they have found someone, the two students then work together to prepare a short talk on why they enjoy that particular hobby.

Additional activity 6

Pairwork: Make enough copies of photocopiable page 6 for each pair, and cut them into parts A and B. Using the cues in the left-hand column of their table, students make questions to ask each other for the information they need. They then work together to pair up the six people as penfriends, on the basis of similar likes and dislikes. (Answers: Becky and Sam, Joanne and Maria, Ahmet and Paul.)

⬤ Think about it!

(Student's Book page 31)

These sections are a basic round-up of the language taught in the unit. They can be done individually or in pairs in class, or for homework, then checked in the next lesson.

Answers

1 **b** 2 **c** 5 **d** 1 **e** 4

2 *Students' own answers*

3 **b** need to **c** needn't **d** need to
e needn't

4 *Students' own answers*

Workbook answers

❶

2 Peter makes model aeroplanes.
3 Jack collects badges.
4 Lynn plays chess.
5 William plays the piano.
6 Joanna plays football.
7 Sally collects stamps.
8 Chris goes horse-riding.

❷

2 Join the collectors club.
3 Join the sports and games club.
4 Join the penfriends club.
5 Join the arts and crafts club.
6 Join the music society.
7 Join the drama society.
8 Join the sports and games club.

❸ *Students' own answers*

❹

3 You don't have to / needn't buy expensive trainers.
4 You have to / need to enjoy physical exercise.
5 You have to / need to fill in a form.
6 You have to / need to enjoy writing letters.
7 You don't have to / needn't speak a foreign language.
8 You don't have to / needn't have a very big collection.
9 You have to / need to enjoy finding things.
10 You have to / need to bring your collection when you join.

❺

(Possible answers)
In the library
You don't have to / needn't pay.
You have to / need to bring your books back on time.

At school
You have to / need to study.
You have to / need to do homework.
You don't have to / needn't go on Sunday.

In a restaurant or café
You don't have to / needn't eat three courses.
You have to / need to pay the bill.
You have to / need to order from the waiter or waitress.

At the cinema
You have to / need to buy a ticket.
You don't have to / needn't be smart.
You have to / need to be quiet.

6

(Possible answers)

Things you can collect	**Things you can make**
coins	models
badges	badges
stamps	clothes
dolls	jewellery
stones	posters

Sports and games	**Musical instruments**
football	violin
horse-riding	piano
aerobics	flute
chess	clarinet
gymnastics	guitar

7

1 have to / need to
2 have to / need to
3 have to / need to
4 have to / need to
5 don't have to / needn't
6 don't have to / needn't

Buzz words

a coins b stamps c jewellery d cans e badges
f comics g matchboxes

8

You have to:
decide what to collect

You need to:
decide on something you enjoy or are already
interested in
choose a theme

You don't have to / needn't:
spend a lot of money
meet with other people who collect the same things

9

(Possible answers)
First, you have to live near the sea, and be interested
in sea life.

Next, you need to clean the shells, and have a place
to display them.

Finally, you don't have to / needn't know much about
the sea and you don't have to / needn't spend any
money.

A day in the life

Active vocabulary

advantage	brush (*verb*)	disadvantage
discussion	entrance	famous
normal	office	rest (*noun*)
restaurant	set (*noun*)	shower (*noun*)
studio	wardrobe department	

Receptive vocabulary

armchair	article	caption
charity	comic (*adjective*)	conclusion
daily	dressing room	equivalent
film star	guest	gunge
interview	iron (*verb*)	mess
office party	personally	plastic
pretty (*adverb*)	recent	rehearsal
routine	salad	security guard
silly	similar	technique
teenager		

Materials

Prepare a sheet of paper divided in two with half sentences on each half. The first half should include *have* and an adverb of frequency and the second half should have a time and place phrase. For example:

I normally have a shower   in the morning at home.
I usually have a drink   in the afternoon at school.

Cut the sentences in half to form cards. Pairs will use these for Additional activity 1.

Copies of photocopiable page 7 for Additional activity 3.

Lead-in

Tell the class about your daily routine on a normal day, for example, *I get up, brush my teeth and have a shower in the morning.* Ask students what they do at different times of the day. On the board try to build up a picture of one or two different daily routines.

Vocabulary

(Student's Book page 32)

Exercise 1

- Ask students to look at the pictures of Jenny's daily routine in the Student's Book. Elicit the key verbs and phrases for her daily routine (*has a shower, has breakfast, arrives at work, meets the director, irons clothes, rehearses, interviews, has a cup of tea*) and check comprehension.

- Introduce the character Jenny to students and ask them how old they think she is (approximately). What do they think she does? What do they think she is interested in? What does she enjoy doing?

- a: Read the instructions for question a, and ask students to look at the list of places Jenny goes to during the course of her day. They must look at the pictures of Jenny and decide where she is in each picture.

- Check students understand most of the words. You can give them some guidance on techniques they can use to help them guess any words they are unsure of (see b below). Give the students a few minutes to do this.

- Go round the class and check answers.

Answers

1 bathroom   2 kitchen   3 entrance   4 office
5 wardrobe department   6 restaurant   7 studio
8 on the set   9 dressing room

- b: Ask students how they worked out the meaning of each word in a. Go through the list of techniques here and ask if they used any of these. If they did, they can tick them.

- Now see if students have used any techniques of their own and add them to this list, encouraging them to share their ideas with the rest of the class.

Additional activity 1

Give out the prepared cards with half-sentences on (see Materials on page 39). The students each take a card and go round the class, reading their half-sentence to each other until they can match up with someone else to form a sensible sentence.

Exercise 2

- In pairs, students look at the pictures in Exercise 1 again, focusing on what Jenny is doing.

- Go through the example with them. Ask them where Jenny is in picture 2 (*the kitchen*) and what she is doing (*eating her breakfast*). Elicit the time of day (*early in the morning*).

- Students now go through the remaining pictures and decide what time of day it is and what Jenny is doing. Encourage them to use the present continuous tense in their answers.

Answers

1 It's early in the morning. She's brushing her teeth.
2 It's early in the morning. She's eating breakfast.
3 It's early in the morning. She's arriving at work.
4 It's late in the morning. She's meeting the director.
5 It's late in the morning. She's looking at clothes.
6 It's lunchtime. She's eating her lunch.
7 It's the afternoon. She's rehearsing.
8 It's the afternoon. She's interviewing someone.
9 It's late in the afternoon. She's drinking a cup of tea.

Exercise 3

- a: Look at the list of phrases on page 32 with the students. Focus on the examples, explaining that *have breakfast* and *eat breakfast* mean the same thing.

- Students now go through the other expressions in the chart and find alternative ways of expressing the meaning.

- b: Students look at the pictures of Jenny and use the phrases they have learnt here to describe them again. Encourage students to use *have* expressions where possible. Do an example with them if necessary.

Exercise 4

- a: Go through the table with students, pointing out the time phrases, the place phrases and the action phrases.

- Explain that they must make more notes in the table based on their own daily routines (what they do and where they do them). Give them time to complete their tables.

- b: In pairs or groups, students use the information in their tables to talk about their daily routines. Ask a few more confident students to read out their routines to the class.

Additional activity 2

Students can mime daily routine activities at the front of the class and the others must guess what they are doing and when they are doing it.

Additional activity 3

Pairwork: Make enough copies of photocopiable page 2 for each pair, and cut them into parts A and B. Using the cues in the left-hand column of their table, students ask questions to get information about their partner's job. If they can't guess the answer, encourage them to follow up with other questions of their own.

Language focus

(Student's Book page 33)

Exercise 1

* Ask students if they can remember what Jenny's normal daily routine is. Then get them to compare these pictures of Jenny last Thursday and ask them what was different from her normal routine. Elicit a few answers, for example, *She wore a red nose.*
* Students work in pairs or groups and decide what the other differences are.

Exercise 2

* In pairs, students read the photo captions that Jenny has written and match them to the photos. Do the first one with the class as an example.

Answers
a 5 b 3 c 1 d 4 e 2

Exercise 3

* Look at the table on page 33 with the students.
* Explain that the first column refers to Jenny's normal daily routine and that the second column refers to the special Comic Relief Day events.
* Elicit one difference from students, for example, *She usually arrives at work before 9 but on Thursday she arrived late.*
* Students read the captions for the photos again and make notes in their tables, building up a contrast of the two days.

Focus

* Students look at their notes from Exercise 3 again. Ask them which tense they used to describe Jenny's normal day. Elicit *the present simple* and write an example on the board. Students write the example sentence in their books.
* Do the same for Jenny's unusual day, eliciting the answer *the past simple* and an example sentence. Ask students how they form the past simple of regular verbs. Draw attention to the example *I missed my bus* and elicit the answer: *Base form + -ed.*
* Remind students of irregular past tense verbs. Ask them to match the verbs with their past forms in the box. Students go through the photo captions again in Exercise 2 and find more examples of irregular past tense verbs.

Additional activity 4

Play 'Past tense bingo' with students. Ask them to make a bingo card with a selection of verbs in the infinitive. Read out the past tense of the selected verbs in random order. The student who first covers all their infinitives correctly is the winner.

Exercise 4

* In pairs or groups, students use their notes from Exercise 3 and talk about Jenny's normal day and her unusual day.

Exercise 5

* Ask students if they can think of any special days which occur during the year when they have a different routine. Elicit some examples and write them on the board. Then ask them to think of a special or unusual day which happened at school.
* a and b: Students make notes individually about their normal daily routine compared with this special or unusual day. In pairs, they talk about this with their partner. Monitor to ensure that they are using present and past tenses correctly.
* c: Students write a short article based on their notes. (Refer them to Jenny's captions in Exercise 2, if necessary.) You could ask them to read out their articles to the class. They can also add pictures or drawings to their articles if they want, and the more interesting ones can be displayed on the classroom wall.

Skills focus

(Student's Book page 34)

Exercise 1

- Set the scene by referring the students to the photo and asking them what they think is happening. Who is in the picture? Why is Jenny talking to the teenager? What do they think his job might be? Why do they think he is famous?

Exercise 2 🔲 ❶

- Refer the students to the questions on the page and say they are going to hear an interview and must listen for the answers to the questions.

- Go over the answers with the class.

🔲 **TAPESCRIPT**

Jenny Hello, and welcome to 'The Biz'. I'm Jenny Wheeler, and today I'm talking to the actor Chet Walker. He's only thirteen years old, but he's already a big star. Chet, welcome to the show.

Chet Thanks.

Jenny Chet, I expect you lead a really exciting life, don't you?

Chet Well, not really. I mean, most of the time, my life is pretty normal. I go to school, I go out with my friends occasionally …

Jenny In Los Angeles?

Chet That's right. I live in Los Angeles, in the USA.

Jenny And most of the time, your life there is normal.

Chet Yes, it is! I do homework …

Jenny Do you enjoy that?

Chet No, not really. But I have to do it, just like everyone else.

Jenny But last month was different, wasn't it?

Chet Yes, it was. I made a new movie. It's called 'Back Home'.

Jenny And what was your life like last month?

Chet Really different! For example, I didn't go to school. I spent every day in the studio.

Jenny Great! So, no school work.

Chet Well, I still had to do school work. But I did it in the evenings. So I didn't see my friends at all.

Jenny That doesn't sound so good!

Chet No, it wasn't. I mean, it's great making movies, but there are disadvantages, too. It's not all fun.

Jenny No, I suppose not. I'd like to ask you some more questions about that. You know, the good things and the bad things about being a child star.

Chet OK. Ask me anything you like …

Answers

a   Chet Walker lives in Los Angeles.

b   Last month he made a new movie.

c   The rest of the interview is going to be about the advantages and disadvantages of making movies.

Look!

- Show students the different word for *film* in American English: *movie*. Ask them if they can think of any other words which are different in English and American English.

Exercise 3

- a: Students listen to the cassette again and complete the chart. Go over the answers with the class.

Answers	
Normally	**Last month**
goes to school	made a movie
sees friends during the day	spent every day in the studio
does school work during the day	didn't see friends at all
	did school work every evening

- b: Students work in pairs making sentences comparing what Chet does normally with what he did last month. Go through the example with them.

- Go over the answers with the class.

Exercise 4

- Students think about what they might hear in the rest of the interview, and complete the list of questions in their books.

Exercise 5 🔲 ❷

- a: Play item 2. Students listen and check their answers to Exercise 4. Play the cassette a second time, pausing if necessary after each question.

- b: Play item 2 again. Students listen and note Chet's answers to their questions.

- c: In pairs or groups, students discuss the advantages and disadvantages of Chet's life as a film star. Ask them to make notes in a table, which will be used in Exercise 6.

TAPESCRIPT

Jenny So, Chet, you mentioned your friends in Los Angeles.

Chet That's right.

Jenny Do you spend much time with your friends?

Chet Well, not really. I'm so busy, you see, I haven't really got time. It's a shame.

Jenny Do you have to work in the evenings?

Chet Yes, I do. I mean, I've always got lots of school work to do. And I also have to learn my lines.

Jenny Do you make any new friends when you're filming?

Chet Not really. Most of the other people in the studio are adults.

Jenny I see.

Chet I don't really spend much time with people my own age.

Jenny I understand. But there must be some good things about being a film star. Do you earn a lot of money?

Chet Money? Well, I suppose so, yes.

Jenny That's good!

Chet Yes, it is.

Jenny And what about travel. Do you travel a lot?

Chet Yes, I do. I get to see other countries. Like England, for example!

Jenny Of course. What do you think of London? …

Exercise 6

- Ask B students to imagine they are going to interview a film star and to prepare some questions. Go round helping with these questions if necessary.

- Ask A students to complete the fact file about themselves in their role of film star. They will use this information to answer Student B's questions.

- In pairs, the students ask and answer questions.

Exercise 7

- a: In groups, students discuss the advantages and disadvantages of being famous.

- b: Students read through the list of expressions. Ask students if they can add any more expressions to the lists.

- c: What do they think? Ask each group for their opinions about being famous and invite other students to reply.

⬤ Think about it!

(Student's Book page 35)

These sections are a basic round-up of the language taught in the unit. They can be done individually or in pairs in class, or for homework, then checked in the next lesson.

Answers

1 **b** discussion **c** lunch **d** drink **e** rest
2 ran, decided, felt, collected
3 arrived, decided, collected
4 *Students' own answers*
5 *Students' own answers*
6 **a** present simple **b** past simple

Workbook answers

❶

2 in the office
3 in the kitchen
4 in the bathroom
5 in the wardrobe department
6 in the dressing room

❷

2 She's having lunch.
3 She's having a cup of tea.
4 She's having breakfast.
5 She's having a business meeting.
6 She's having a rest.

❸

(Possible answers)

studio	**office**
chair	chair
table	table
computer	computer
camera	telephone
telephone	door
door	window
window	
microphone	

dressing room	**bathroom**
chair	mirror
table	shower
mirror	door
door	window
window	
clothes	

kitchen	**entrance**
fridge	door
chair	
table	
door	
window	

❹

2 At half past seven she has breakfast.

3 From eight o'clock to half past twelve, she has lessons.

4 From quarter to one to half past one, she has lunch.

5 From half past one to four o'clock, she has more lessons.

6 From four o'clock to five o'clock, she has a break.

7 From five o'clock to seven o'clock, she does homework.

8 From seven o'clock to quarter to eight, she has dinner.

9 From quarter to eight to quarter to ten, she talks to friends, watches TV and plays games.

10 At quarter to ten she gets ready for bed.

11 At quarter past ten she goes to sleep.

❺

2	had	11	arrived	20	left
3	got	12	ran	21	sang
4	was	13	went	22	laughed
5	woke	14	felt	23	fell
6	had	15	came	24	got
7	went	16	ate	25	went
8	started	17	decided	26	was
9	travelled	18	was	27	had
10	stopped	19	saw		

❻

Base form	Past form
begin	had
need	wanted
taste	sat
decide	found
	wore
	was/were

❼

2 have; discuss

3 see; talked

4 collected; don't do

5 ate; wore; wear

6 eat; had

7 go; fell

Buzz words

1 started

2 went

3 came

4 studied

5 arrived

6 wanted

7 covered

The hidden word is *decided*.

Dictionary skills

1 4   2 6   3 2   4 1   5 3   6 5

❽

2 He has dinner at 3.00 in the morning.

3 He goes to school at 8.00 in the evening.

4 He does his homework at 7.30 in the morning.

5 He has a wash at 7.15 in the evening.

6 He watches TV until 11.30 in the morning.

❾ *Students' own answers*

One step at a time

Learning objectives

- talking about different jobs
- learning about how a magazine is produced
- talking about how things are done

Language focus

- present passive

Active vocabulary

bite	caption	chase
column	copy (*noun*)	creative
designer	distribute	edge
editor	fold	frighten
heading	illustration	line
magazine	mosquito	paragraph
picture researcher	print (*verb*)	reporter
sew	stick	storm
team	trap (*verb*)	voice
win		

Receptive vocabulary

add	animated film	department
direct (*verb*)	edit	indoors
issue	key (*verb*)	layout
model	pack (*verb*)	photographer
picture library	print-out	printer
process	prompt (*noun*)	record (*verb*)
scenery	sound effect	synonym

Materials

If possible, bring in a teen magazine for Lead-in b.

Some dice and counters for the Skills focus board game.

Copies of photocopiable page 8 for Additional activity 3.

Lead-ins

a Revise the difference between what we do habitually with what we are doing now. Say, *I usually teach. I am teaching English now. What about you?* A student gives two sentences about himself/herself and asks the next person. Continue in a chain round the room.

b Ask the students to look at the picture of the teen magazine on page 36, or show them an authentic magazine if you have brought one in. Elicit or give the words for the different parts of the page (*paragraph*, *heading*, *photo*, *illustration*, *column*, *caption*, *line*), getting students to repeat after you. Write the words on the board.

Ask students what kind of information articles and features they might put in a teen magazine. Ask how they could make the magazine interesting (include photos and illustrations, cartoons, interviews, etc.).

Vocabulary

(Student's Book page 36)

Exercise 1

- Talk about the fact that schools often produce school magazines. Ask if the students have ever done this or thought about doing this themselves. Listen to any ideas they might have.
- Students look at the picture of the teen magazine on page 12. Ask them what sort of magazine they think the page comes from.
- Elicit the types of magazines that they like to read and ask what makes them interesting.

Exercise 2

- Give the students a few minutes to study the magazine page and complete the exercise.

Answers

caption 7   column 2   heading 1   illustration 3
paragraph 5   photo 6   line 4

▶ **Note**

Point out the difference between a photo and an illustration.

Exercise 3

- Give the students a few moments to study the pictures of the people numbered 1–4. Ask what they know about each of these jobs. They probably will not have a very clear idea of what editors, designers and picture researchers do, but elicit ideas and suggestions and ask them to say what they think is going on in each picture.

Exercise 4

- Students read the descriptions of the jobs and match the descriptions to the people in Exercise 3. Remind students to think about the techniques they are using to match the people with the descriptions. Give help with any vocabulary problems.

Answers

a   Tim Stern, reporter
b   Lisa Ryan, editor
c   Rebecca Farrell, picture researcher
d   Amanda Cooke, designer

Exercise 5

- Students read the sentences again and think about the techniques they used to find their answers in Exercise 4. Read through the list of techniques with them. Did they use any of these?
- Point out the words in bold in paragraph a and go through the example with them. Ask students which techniques can be used to predict the meanings of the other words.

Answers

copy: technique a. There is a a synonym in commas after the word ('copy, or text,').

edit: technique b. The meaning is explained in the next few words ('this means that ... necessary changes').

picture library: technique c.

layout: technique b. The meaning is explained in the next few words ('that is, what they will look like').

Exercise 6

- Students work in pairs or groups. They think about the people who work on the magazine and decide which person has the most interesting and creative job and which person has the least interesting job. Allow students time to discuss this as a whole class.

Additional activity 1

Students decide which magazine job they find the most interesting and write about why they like it. Remind them they can use *I enjoy + -ing* or *I am interested in*, or the present simple. They then read their reasons to their partner who guesses which job it is.

Language focus

(Student's Book page 37)

Exercise 1

- Ask students to look at the flow chart and decide what it shows. Provide help with any vocabulary they may need to understand the chart: *keyed in, passed on, film, print, printer, produced, packed, distributed*.

Answer

It shows the different stages of making/producing the magazine.

Exercise 2

- Individually or in pairs, students read the list of captions and decide in which order the events take place in the process of producing the magazine.

Answers

a 3   b 2   c 5   d 6   e 1   f 4

Focus

- Students think about and compare the texts they read in Vocabulary (page 36) and Language focus (page 37). They answer the questions in their book.

Answers

a   the people who produce the magazine – Vocabulary text

b   the process/stages of producing the magazine – Language focus chart and pictures

- Look at the example sentence in the Focus box with students, particularly the verb forms in bold. Explain that these verb forms are describing the stages of a process.

▶ **Note**

Point out that *are chosen* is a plural form and *is designed* is a singular form.

- Students look at the captions in Exercise 2 again and find other examples of the passive (*be* + past participle).
- Explain the structure of the passive to students and go through the chart of regular and irregular examples in the book.
- Students now find examples of past participles in the captions in Exercise 2 and add them to the chart in the book. They then complete the chart by filling in the base forms and the past forms.

Exercise 3

- Students look at the chart and the list of words on page 37 describing the various stages of book production. In pairs or groups, they describe the process. Remind them to use the passive construction when they are describing the process and to watch for the difference between singular and plural forms.
- Students can read out their descriptions to the rest of the class.

Exercise 4

- Students think about the process of book production before the pages are printed. They can use all the information they have learnt from this unit so far to discuss what happens. Ask them to work in groups and encourage them to use the passive.

◯ Skills focus

(Student's Book page 38)

Exercise 1

- Refer students to the photo of Tim Stern interviewing Ricky Jones. Read questions a and b and elicit answers.

Answers

a   Ricky Jones directs animated films.

b   Max is one of the models he uses in his films.

Exercise 2 ▭ ❶

- Refer students to the chart and choose a student to read out the jobs in the left-hand column. Explain that as they listen to the cassette, they should tick the middle column if Ricky does the job mentioned, and the right-hand column if somebody else does it.
- Demonstrate by pausing the cassette at the end of Ricky's words, 'first of all, the story is written'. Ask *Who writes the story?* and elicit the point that we don't know – no person is mentioned here. Play on to the end of Ricky's next speech, pause again and ask *Who writes the stories – Ricky?* Elicit the answer no – they *are written by* a team of writers and so the tick should go in the right-hand column.
- Play the conversation through and ask students to compare their answers in pairs or small groups. Then play the cassette again.
- Check answers with the whole class.

▭ **TAPESCRIPT**

Tim   So, Ricky, tell me about your films.

Ricky   Well, as you know, I make animated films.

Tim   But not cartoons.

Ricky   No, not cartoons. My films are made with models – like Max here.

Tim   And how exactly are the films made? Can you explain it simply?

Ricky   Of course. Well, first of all, the story is written.

Tim   And do you write all the stories?

Ricky   No, I don't. In fact, all the stories are written by a team of writers. When a story is finished, I'm given a copy of the script.

Tim	And then you make the film?
Ricky	Well, yes … but lots of things need to be done first. For example, the models need to be made.
Tim	Do you do that?
Ricky	No, I don't. All the models are made by my assistant, Carole. She's good with her hands.
Tim	So, Carole makes all the models. Then what?
Ricky	Then all the scenery is painted.
Tim	By Carole?
Ricky	No, we have a team of artists to do that.
Tim	I see. What happens next?
Ricky	Then we make the film. The models are placed in front of the scenery and a single frame of film is photographed.
Tim	Who operates the camera? Is that your job?
Ricky	No, the camera is operated by the cameraman.
Tim	Yes, of course.
Ricky	Then the models are moved just a tiny bit and another frame of film is photographed. Then they're moved again … and so on. This is repeated hundreds and hundreds of times to make the film.
Tim	Does Carole move the models each time?
Ricky	Yes, she does.
Tim	And then the film's finished?
Ricky	Nearly. The voices are recorded …
Tim	Who does …
Ricky	… by actors, of course. And then sound effects are added by Nigel, our sound effects man. And then it's finished! And the film can be enjoyed by children and adults all over the world.
Tim	Great! And what exactly do *you* do?
Ricky	Well, I'm the director. I'm in charge …

Answers

All the ticks should be in the 'somebody else' column.

Focus

- Read the Focus box to the class. Allow students to answer the questions if they can.

Answers

- The underlined words tell us who does the action.

- In the first example, the verb is singular because the subject (*story*) is singular. For the second, the verb is plural because the subject (*sound effects*) is plural.

Exercise 3

- Give students five minutes to complete Tim's notes. Then play the cassette again and allow the students to check their answers.

Answers

The story is written by a team of writers.

The models are made by Carole, Ricky's assistant.

The sound effects are added by Nigel, the sound effects man.

The voices are recorded by actors.

The camera is operated by the cameraman.

The scenery is painted by artists.

The models are moved by Carole, Ricky's assistant.

Additional activity 2

Invite students to interview you about your daily routine, including lesson preparation and marking.

They then write about your day using the passive as much as possible (*The lesson is prepared. The bag is packed. The date is written on the board. The books are collected in. The work is marked*).

Exercise 4

- Students may need ten minutes to write Tim's report for the magazine. Refer them to their answers in Exercise 3 to help them. Go round checking they use the passive.

Additional activity 3

Students might like to plan their own school magazine or English language class magazine. Put them into groups. Each group chooses an editor, a designer and reporters, and a name for their magazine. They must think of some stories and how they will illustrate them. This could be a project they would like to continue.

Pairwork: Make enough copies of photocopiable page 8 for each pair, and cut them into parts A and B. Student A has a scrambled set of sentences and Student B has a set of pictures in the correct order. Give them each a few minutes to look at their sheet, allowing A to look up any unfamiliar words (e.g. sorting office, van). B then describes the events in sequence. A identifies the sentences and numbers the boxes in the right order.

Game

Exercise 1

- Refer students to the board game and read through the text squares to check understanding.

- Students write ten prompts on separate pieces of paper. Go through the ten prompts with them. Explain that the first five prompts are bad things which happen to students in the game and they will miss a turn with these ones: *You are chased by a dog. Miss a go!* The second five are good things and if they happen students have an extra turn: *You win a car. Throw again!*

▶ **Note**

The first five prompts require use of the passive, while the other five require the active.

- In groups, encourage students to think of more prompts to add to the game and ask them to write them down. For example: (bad) *attack/bear*, (good) *find/money*.

Exercise 2

- Give out the dice and counters. Students play together in pairs or groups, reading the text and following the instructions. Remind them that if they land on a square with a question mark, another player must pick up a piece of paper and make a sentence.

◯ **Think about it!**

(Student's Book page 39)

These sections are a basic round-up of the language taught in the unit. They can be done individually or in pairs in class, or for homework, then checked in the next lesson.

Answers

1 **a** page 12   **b** all pages   **c** all pages
   d page 12
2 **b** The text is checked.   **c** The pictures are chosen.   **d** The pages are designed.
3 **a** reporter   **b** editor   **c** picture researcher
   d designer
4 made, moved, chose, sent
5 *Students' own answers*

Workbook answers

❶

2 I choose stories for the photos. (Picture researcher)
3 I sometimes contact the picture library. (Picture researcher)
4 I work on the computer most of the time. (Designer)
5 I design the layout of the pages. (Designer)
6 I arrange the text headings. (Editor)
7 I send the proofs to the printers. (Editor)
8 I interview people. (Reporter)
9 I type the stories into the computer. (Reporter)
10 I give the text to the editor. (Reporter)
11 I read the stories and check them for mistakes. (Editor)
12 I copy the photos and pass them on. (Picture researcher)

Buzz words

1 photo
2 heading
3 column
4 paragraph
5 illustration
6 caption
7 line

❷

check in = to register someone as a guest at a hotel
porter = a person whose job is to carry people's luggage to and from their hotel room
housekeeper = a person who is employed to shop, cook, clean the house, etc.
safety deposit boxes = strong boxes or cupboards with a complicated lock, used for storing valuable things
Students' own answers

❸

Base form	Past form	Past participle
bite (I)	bit	bitten
choose (I)	chose	chosen
meet (I)	met	met
pass (R)	passed	passed
produce (R)	produced	produced
put (I)	put	put
send (I)	sent	sent
spend (I)	spent	spent
stick (I)	stuck	stuck
write (I)	wrote	written

❹

1 is used
2 is called; is pressed; is put
3 is designed
4 are printed; is given
5 are taken
6 are held; replaced
7 are burnt/burned

❺

1 false; line 3/4
2 true; line 6
3 false; lines 7/8
4 false; lines 13/14
5 true; line 15
6 false; lines 18/19

❻

2 Potatoes are grown by farmers.
3 Books are written by authors.
4 Clothes are designed by fashion designers.
5 Paintings are created by artists.
6 Cars are produced by car workers.
7 Bread is made by bakers.
8 Newspaper stories are written by reporters.
9 Restaurant food is cooked by chefs.
10 Flowers are sold by florists.

Dictionary skills

1 magazine
2 noun
3 a magazine article
4 does this magazine

Earth strikes back

Learning objectives

- talking about continuous events in the past
- reading reports about natural disasters
- describing what people were doing when something happened

Language focus

- past continuous
- past simple
- interrupted past: past continuous and past simple

Active vocabulary

active	bowl	earthquake
feed (*verb*)	fisherman	grape
inactive	jug	mend
net	pick	pot
potter	volcano	wheel

Receptive vocabulary

amazingly	ash	casualty
cloud	collapse	enormous
erupt	eruption	field
flash (*noun*)	god	guide (*noun*)
inhabitant	interrupt	invent
kill	lava	lightning
make sense	plan (*noun*)	remains (*noun*)
shock	shout	sudden
tour	valley	village

Materials

Copies of photocopiable page 9 for Additional activity 3.

Lead-ins

a   Revise the language from the previous unit. Ask students to write three sentences in the passive about their favourite sport or hobby.

b   Make a sentence about what someone was doing when you came into the room, for example, *Philip, you were talking when I came into the room.* Now ask questions: *Julia, what were you doing when I came into the room?* Encourage students to reply using *I was + -ing when you came into the room.*

Students ask each other what they were doing half an hour ago, making a chain around the class

For example:

A   (*I was talking. What were you doing?*

B   *Andrea was talking, I was doing my homework. What were you doing?*).

C   *Andrea was talking, Kim was doing his homework and I was ...*

Ask students to tell you about a famous event during the last few years. Can the class remember what they were doing when it happened?

Vocabulary

(Student's Book page 40)

Background

Herculaneum was a small ancient Roman town on the lower slopes of Vesuvius, whose eruption in AD 79 buried and preserved it as it was. From Herculaneum and its more famous neighbour Pompeii, we have been able to learn a lot about life in Roman times, including what people ate, what they wore, how they farmed and travelled.

Exercise 1

- Refer students to the picture of Herculaneum and ask them to read the text.

- a: Read the question. Students say what they think the difference is between an active and an inactive volcano. Ask them if they can think of any active volcanoes in existence. (Vesuvius is still active, as is Etna, also in Italy; Other active volcanoes incude Hekla in Iceland, Mauna Kea in Hawaii, Popocatepetl in Mexico and Erebus in Antarctica.)

- b: Students tell you which words they think are missing from the text (*verbs*). Ask them how they came to their decisions – what techniques did they use?

- c: Students go through the text again and try and guess which words complete the gaps. (They should not fill in the gaps at this point.) Encourage them to look at the sentences surrounding the gaps to help them.

Exercise 2 🎞 ❶

- Students listen to item 1 and complete the gaps in the text with the words they hear. Check their answers, and ask them to use the questions to re-assess their predictions fom Exercise 1c. There are various alternatives that could fit each of the gaps, and students should not think they are 'wrong' if they thought of a different verb in the correct tense and with an appropriate meaning.

🎞 TAPESCRIPT

Volcanoes are named after Vulcan, the Roman god of fire. Most volcanoes are inactive, but an active volcano can suddenly become a mountain of fire. When a volcano erupts, the lava and ash can destroy towns and villages, and kill the people who live there.

The first well-recorded eruption was that of Vesuvius in ad 79. It buried the Roman towns of Pompeii and Herculaneum, and killed 16,000 people. A Roman writer, Pliny the Younger, saw the eruption. He wrote about the 'horrible black cloud' and 'sudden flashes, larger than lightning'.

Exercise 3

- Refer students again to the picture of Herculaneum and ask them to give you as much vocabulary as they can about what they see.

- Read the question. Students say how they know it is a town in the past.

Suggested answers

Style of clothes and buildings, no cars, no electricity or telephone cables, no modern machinery, the vessels they use for carrying water.

Exercise 4

- a: Read through the prompts on page 40. Ask students to look at the picture of Herculaneum and find the fisherman. Ask what he is doing and elicit the sentence given in the example.

- Students then match the other prompts with the pictures and write them out as full sentences in their notebooks, following the example. (Answers will be checked in Exercise 5.)

Answers

a 6 A woman is feeding some/her chickens.
b 2 A girl is picking grapes.
c 1 A fisherman is mending his nets.
d 5 Women are carrying jugs of water.
e 4 A potter is making a bowl.
f 3 A man is mending a wheel.

- b: Give students a few minutes to talk in pairs about other actions taking place in the picture. Monitor to make sure that they are using the present continuous construction correctly.

Answers

A boy is pointing.
Two children are playing with a ball.
A cat is sleeping.
A dog is eating.
A woman is cooking.
A man is drinking.
Children are running (across a field).
A girl is washing her hair.
A man is carrying (a box of) grapes.
A woman is washing clothes.

Additional activity 1

Students take it in turns to mime one of the actions taking place in the picture and the rest of the class tries to guess what they are doing, for example, *You are mending nets.*

Pronunciation

Exercise 5 ❷

- Play item 2. Students check their answers to Exercise 4a, correcting as necessary.

- Go through the example sentence with the students, pointing out the stress on the words. Ask them to listen to the tape again and mark the stress on the sentences in their notebooks.

- Ask students to look again at their answers and see if they can decide why certain words are stressed while others are not.

📻 TAPESCRIPT

1 A fisherman is mending his nets.
2 A girl is picking grapes.
3 A man is mending a wheel.
4 A potter is making a bowl.
5 Two women are carrying jugs of water.
6 A woman is feeding some chickens.

Answers

b 1 A fisherman is mending his nets.

2 A girl is picking grapes.

3 A man is mending a wheel.

4 A potter is making a bowl.

5 Two women are carrying jugs of water.

6 A woman is feeding some chickens.

c They are the most important words in the sentence – nouns, verbs and numbers (note that adjectives and adverbs are also usually stressed).

◐ Language focus

(Student's Book page 41)

Exercise 1 📻 ❸

- Give students a few minutes to look at the photo of the woman. Ask them what they think her job is and discuss ideas round the class.

- Play item 3 for students to check their answers.

Answer

She is a tour guide.

📻 TAPESCRIPT

Hello, and welcome to Herculaneum. My name's Juliet and I'm going to be your guide for the afternoon. We're going to have a walk around some of the amazing ruins here. As you know, when Vesuvius erupted in AD 79, it covered the whole town in lava and ash. By studying the remains, we can work out what everyone was doing at that moment. Follow me.

Exercise 2

- Give students a few minutes to look at the plan of Herculaneum and ask them to tell you what they can see in it.

Answers

The body of a mother and a young child, toys, a wheel, some pots and pans, a plate and some bowls, a potter's wheel, the bodies of a young couple.

Exercise 3 📻 ❹

- Students now listen to the rest of the guided tour (item 4) and find out about the order of the rooms. Ask them to number the rooms on their plan.

Answers

1 The home of the young couple.
2 The home of the mother and child.
3 The home of the potter.

📻 TAPESCRIPT

Here we are in the first room. As you can see, this was probably the home of a young man and his wife. If we look at their bodies, and the other objects in the room, we can work out what they were doing when Vesuvius erupted. We found a wheel next to the man, and some pots and pans near the woman. At the time of the eruption, the man was mending a wheel and his wife was cooking dinner …

And on to the second room. In this room, we found two bodies – a mother and her child. We also found several toys. Obviously, the mother was playing with her child when the eruption happened …

And here we are in the third room. This house belonged to a potter. We found his potter's wheel here, together with lots of plates, bowls, and so on. We can tell from the body that he was making a bowl when the lava and ash covered his home.

Exercise 4

- a: Students look at the young couple's room on their plan. Referring to this, they read the text and fill in the gaps. Remind them to think about what they heard on the tape in Exercise 3.
- b: Play the first part of item 4 again for students to check their answers to Exercise 4a.

Answers

1 doing 2 wheel 3 pots 4 pans 5 mending 6 cooking

Focus

- Look at the two sentences with the students. Ask them which sentence in the diagram is in the past simple tense (*erupted*).
- Students now look at the past continuous verb (*was mending*). See if they can complete the rules about how this tense is formed and how it can be used with the past simple.

Answers

past continuous = the past of *be* (*was* or *were*) + the *-ing* form of the verb

We use the past *continuous* to describe a continuous action in the past. We use the past *simple* for an event which interrupts that continuous action.

Exercise 5

- a: Students are going to continue the tour of Herculaneum. Give them a few minutes to look at the second and third rooms on their plan and make notes about what these rooms contain.
- b: Replay the rest of item 4. Students listen and add to their notes as necessary.
- c: In pairs or groups, students now describe the two rooms and explain what the people were doing when the volcano erupted. Remind them to use the past continuous construction here.

Exercise 6

- Students turn to Vocabulary page 40 again and look at the picture of Herculaneum. Ask a student *What was he/she doing?*, pointing at one of the people in the picture. Elicit a reply, for example, *She was picking grapes.* Repeat with *What were they doing?* and elicit a reply.
- Students continue to do the same in pairs, taking it in turns to ask and answer about the people they are pointing to.

Additional activity 2

Play 'Alibi'. Tell the students you are going to imagine that a robbery took place at school yesterday. Tell the students to imagine they were all at school at the time and must be questioned about what they were doing when the robbery took place.

- Either: give the students time to prepare a few sentences about what they were doing when the robbery took place to convince you they were not the culprit.
- Or: ask two students to go out of the room and plan together what they were doing when the robbery took place. They must think in as much detail as possible. The rest of the class prepare questions to ask the students when they come in one at a time, for example:

What were you wearing?
Who were you with?
What were you doing?
What were you eating?

Any discrepancies between the answers mean the students are guilty!

Skills focus

(Student's Book page 42)

Exercise 1

- Refer students to the picture and elicit as much vocabulary as you can. You may need to give the words *earthquake*, *collapsed*, *buildings* and *disaster*.
- Read the instructions and elicit possible answers to a and b.

Answers

a Sarah Cox is a reporter.
b She is reporting on an earthquake.

Exercise 2

- Students listen to item 5 and check their answers from Exercise 1.

TAPESCRIPT

Good evening, this is Sarah Cox in California reporting for the six o'clock news. I'm here today to talk to the people of Northridge, California which this morning at 9.30 was hit by an earthquake. Luckily, there were few casualties.

Exercise 🔊 ⑥

- Read the names of the people in the list and make sure the students know how to pronounce them. Students then listen to item 6 and tick the names of the people Sarah Cox interviews.

Answers

These names should be ticked:

Rob King   Hannah Green   Antonio Gonzales

🔊 TAPESCRIPT

Sarah	I'm here with Rob King, a postman who was getting ready for work when the earthquake started. Rob, what happened?
Rob	Well, I didn't know what was happening. I was outside mending my bike when I felt the earth moving up and down. I shouted to my brother who was in the kitchen. He was carrying a jug of coffee. He dropped it as he ran outside.
Sarah	Thanks a lot, Rob. Er, excuse me, what's your name?
Hannah	Mrs Hannah Green.
Sarah	Mrs Green, when did you first know about the earthquake?
Hannah	Well, my husband felt it first. He was feeding the cat. He picked up the cat and ran into the bathroom where I was washing my hair. We could see the buildings shaking. I think it's the worst earthquake in 10 years.
Sarah	What do you think, sir? Could you tell us your name?
Antonio	I'm Antonio Gonzales. I live on a farm outside Northridge. I was picking oranges when it started. I could hear my children shouting. They were playing not far away. They were terrified. There was some damage to the farmhouse but luckily no one was hurt.
Sarah	Thank you, Antonio. Let's go over and talk to one of the rescue teams …

Exercise 4

- Students listen to item 6 again and make notes in the columns in the table.

Answers

	Who?	At time of earthquake
a	Rob King	mending bike
b	his brother	carrying jug of coffee in kitchen
c	Hannah Green	washing hair
d	her husband	feeding cat
e	Antonio Gonzales	picking oranges
f	his children	playing outside

Exercise 5

- In pairs, students tell each other what each person was doing at the time of the earthquake, using their notes from the previous exercise. Monitor to make sure they are using the past continuous correctly.

- With the whole class, pick people from the list in any order and ask students to say what they were doing.

Exercise 6

- Students imagine they live in Northridge. Ask them to write about what they and their families were doing at the time of the earthquake. Give an example on the board: *I was getting ready for school. My mum and dad were having breakfast.*

Exercise 7

- Students work in pairs. Student A is a reporter, Student B an inhabitant of Northridge (B students can use their notes from Exercise 6).

- Give them a few minutes to prepare an interview using the expressions on the page to help them. Point out that the last question is in the past simple and that the answer should also be in this tense. Here we are no longer talking about a continuing 'background' activity, but about a particular action that started and finished at a certain time in the past.

- Volunteers can act out their role-play for the class.

Exercise 8

- a: Students compare the first paragraph of Sarah Cox's article with their notes from Exercise 4. They should notice three discrepancies.

- b: Students look at the second paragraph of the article and fill in the gaps, using their notes from Exercise 4.

Answers

- a   Ron King should be Rob King. His brother was carrying a jug of coffee, not a jug of tea. Rob King was mending his bike, not his car.

- b   Green; hair; husband; feeding; picking; were playing

- c: Students now continue the third paragraph of the article. They should write about the character they invented in Exercise 7. Provide any help needed with vocabulary.
- Students can read out their new paragraphs to the class.

Additional activity 3

Pairwork: Make enough copies of photocopiable page 9 for each pair, and cut them into parts A and B. Students take it in turns to identify the people in the picture by asking each other what each person on their list was doing at the time of the earthquake. The man most likely to be the thief is Steve Smith.

Additional activity 4

Students write a newspaper report about a natural disaster, a crime or another important event that has taken place locally. The event can be imaginary, but the report must include interviews with people, asking them what they were doing at the time. Students could use local papers to get ideas for stories.

◯ Think about it!

(Student's Book page 43)

These sections are a basic round-up of the language taught in the unit. They can be done individually or in pairs in class, or for homework, then checked in the next lesson.

Answers

1 **b** Sarah was making a model.
  c Tim was feeding the cat.
  d Anna was mending a bowl.
  e Mike and Melanie were watching TV.
  f Sue was cleaning the bathroom.
2 **a** was cooking **b** started

Workbook answers

❶

1 VOLCANO ERUPTS! 2 lava 3 cloud ash 4 village

❷

2 They are picking grapes.
3 They are making bowls.
4 The women are feeding chickens.
5 The men are mending fishing nets.
6 The women are washing clothes in a river.
7 The children are playing football in the street.
8 The man is sleeping in the sun.

Dictionary skills

destroy: to damage sth. so badly that it can no longer be used or no longer exists; kill: to make somebody/sth. die; bury: to cover or hide

1 destroy: 2nd syllable; bury: 1st syllable
2 verbs; v

❸

2 Mrs Ashford was sunbathing.
3 John and Maria were swimming.
4 Mr and Mrs Green were buying souvenirs.
5 Harry and Melvin were playing volleyball.
6 Jane and Belinda were cycling.
7 Mr Smith was reading a newspaper.
8 Mrs Hancock was listening to a Walkman.

❹

2 He was watching TV, when the pictures fell off the wall.
3 He was talking on the phone, when the floor fell in.
4 He was sitting in the garden, when a ladder hit his head.
5 He was having a cup of coffee, when the cat jumped on him.
6 He was cooking dinner, when a fire started.
7 He was reading a book, when the ceiling fell down.

❺ *Students' own answers*

❻

2 received	5 was working	8 was eating
3 quickly arrived	6 happened	9 saw
4 went home	7 was making	10 ran

❼

Ann Leeman, a teacher at the school, was teaching when the helicopter crashed. She said, 'It was very frightening! I saw something very big in the playground and then I heard a crash!' Edward Lightfoot, the headmaster, was talking to two students when he heard the crash. He ran out of the office, and told the children to stay in their classrooms. 10-year-old Jeremy Pixman, a student, was reading in the library when he heard the helicopter come down. He sat under a table.

The school will be/stay closed until next week.

Looking after the Earth

Learning objectives

- talking about what things are made from
- thinking about how we can look after the environment
- talking about cause and effect
- expressing opinions about right and wrong

Language focus

- *should* and *shouldn't* to express what is right and wrong

Active vocabulary

aluminium	cotton	energy
environment	fur	glass (*material*)
ivory	jar	leather
leather bag	plastic	pollute
pollution	recycle	should/shouldn't
throw away	waste (*verb*)	wood/wooden
wool/woollen		

Receptive vocabulary

accountant	a drop in the ocean	
aluminium foil	avoid	battery
can (*noun*)	carton	chemical (*noun*)
chopsticks	close friend	container
crazy	destroy	eccentric
endangered	fearless	forest
garbage	garbage can	handkerchief
harm (*verb*)	health	journey
material	napkin	neighbour
next door	packaging	pay a price
questionnaire	re-use	rechargeable
rubbish	stomach	tap
turn off	unnecessary	

Materials

A collection of familiar classroom objects (books, paper, pencils, pens, rubbers) for Lead-in a.

If possible, some authentic objects made from the materials in Vocabulary Exercise 2 (a cotton handkerchief, a glass bottle, etc.).

Copies of photocopiable page 10 for Additional activity 4.

Large pieces of paper (A3) for Skills focus Exercise 5.

Lead-ins

a   Collect together some familiar classroom objects such as books, pencils, pens. Hold them up and elicit vocabulary.

Ask *What is this made of?* holding up an exercise book. Elicit *paper*. Ask *What is paper made of?* Students might answer with *trees* or *wood*.

Ask the students to spend a few minutes writing down the things the other objects are made of. Give any vocabulary they ask for, and have a class discussion, to see if everyone agrees about what each thing is made of.

b   Write *handkerchief* on the board. Students have two minutes to write as many words as they can using the letters from the word, for example, *hand*, *chief*, *and*, *neck*, etc.

Vocabulary

(Student's Book page 44)

Exercise 1

It is generally agreed that we need to look after the world's resources and recycle more materials. Students may have their own knowledge about which materials can be recycled (e.g. paper, aluminium, glass) and which cannot (e.g. plastic).

- Ask students if they do anything to help the environment. Elicit some examples.
- Students now look at the pictures of the people and read the texts about things people do to help the environment. Give help with vocabulary, particularly words for the materials that things are made of.
- Read through questions a to f with the students and ask for examples to demonstrate the meaning of *energy*, *pollution* and *rubbish*.
- Students then match the questions with the correct texts and pictures.
- Ask students if they have done any of these things or would consider doing them.

Answers

a 5   b 2   c 1   d 4   e 6   f 3

Exercise 2

- a: Refer students to the pictures and go over the vocabulary. If you have any authentic objects, show them to the students and let them pass them round.
- Read the instructions. Students try to match each object with the material it is made from. Check answers with the class.

Answers

1	wooden/plastic chopsticks	6	glass bottle
2	cotton T-shirt	7	aluminium can
3	woollen jumper	8	leather bag
4	wooden table	9	leather shoe
5	plastic container		

- b: Students now think of other things they may find at home or at school which are made of the materials in a. Give them a few examples if necessary (e.g. *wooden desk*).
- c: Students now think about recycling and discuss what sort of things they can recycle or re-use in a different way.

Word grammar

Exercise 3

- Check that students understand that a noun is a naming word for a person or thing. An adjective is a describing word which tells us more about that person or thing.
- Some words can be an adjective or a noun, e.g. *a paper cup* (*paper* is an adjective), *Give me the paper* (*paper* is a noun).
- Students read the words in the table and focus on the underlined words. Elicit the adjective *wooden* from the noun *wood* and ask for an example to go in column 2 (e.g. *wooden chairs*). Do the same in reverse to elicit an example for *wool* in column 1 (e.g. *wool grows on sheep*).
- Students add more words to the table from the words they have already met in this lesson.

Example answers

Noun	Adjective
ivory comes from elephants	ivory buttons
the fur of an animal	a fur coat
a belt made of leather	a leather belt
aluminium is a metal	aluminium cans
a dress made of cotton	a cotton shirt
a piece of paper	paper plates
the glass is broken	a glass bowl

Wooden and *woollen* are the two adjectives that are different from their nouns.

Language focus

(Student's Book page 45)

Exercise 1

- First pre-teach any unfamiliar vocabulary (e.g. *napkin, re-chargeable, tap, chemicals, packaging, man-made*).

- Students read the questionnaire and decide if the actions listed are the right thing to do or the wrong thing to do in order to help save the environment. They should put a tick or a cross accordingly.

- Ask for class feedback and see if they agree on the right and wrong things to do.

Exercise 2

- Read through the headings with the students. Then ask them to read the questionnaire again and choose a heading for each section of the questionnaire. (Do the first one with them as an example if necessary.)

Answers

1 Save trees
2 Don't waste water or energy
3 Don't cause pollution
4 Don't create rubbish
5 Protect endangered animals

Focus

- Read the two instructions and give the students a few minutes to write two more examples for each.

- Then ask them to complete the sentences. Choose a student to feed back his or her answers and write the missing words on the board.

- Point out that the form of *should* and *shouldn't* is always the same, regardless of the subject (e.g. *I/he/they should/shouldn't*).

Answers

We can use *should* to talk about what we think is the right thing to do.

We can use *shouldn't* to talk about what we think is the wrong thing to do.

Exercise 3

- Students look at the answers they ticked or crossed in the questionnaire and now make sentences with *should* or *shouldn't*.

Additional activity 3

Students work in pairs thinking up some guidelines for the classroom, including guidelines for the teacher. They write these in a list using *should/shouldn't* and read them out to the class. The guidelines can be humorous or serious. You could make a class list to go on the wall, to which each pair contributes one or two of their ideas. For example, *We should only speak English to the teacher. The teacher shouldn't bring her coffee cup into the classroom. We should put rubbish in the bins.*

Exercise 4

- Read the instructions and give students a few minutes to think about why we should or shouldn't do the things the questionnaire suggests. Go through the examples with them.

- Elicit the point that *we'll* = *we will* and establish that we are talking here about the future. However, we can't be sure those things will happen. We are predicting what will happen *if* something else happens first.

- Ask students to predict similar results *if* we do or don't do the things listed in the questionnaire.

Look!

- Draw attention to the two parts of these conditional sentences. Point out that the verb with *if* is in the present simple, while the result verb uses *will*.

Exercise 5

- In pairs, students think of other things we should or shouldn't do to look after the environment and consider the results that will follow otherwise.

- Ask them to write pairs of sentences as in the examples.

Additional activity 4

Pairwork: Make enough copies of photocopiable page 10 for each pair, and cut them into parts A and B. The crossword is about materials and where they come from. Students take it in turn to read out the clues to help their partner work out the missing words. If a student cannot get the right answer from this clue, his/her partner can supply other clues to make it easier. When they have finished, pairs should compare their crosswords, checking that they have both spelt the words correctly.

Skills focus

(Student's Book page 46)

Exercise 1

- Students look at the photos, and read the questions. Working with a partner, they discuss possible answers to the questions and make notes in the middle column of the table. Give students about three minutes to do this, then discuss possible answers with the whole class.

Exercise 2

- Give students ten minutes to read the article and to make notes in the third column of the table. Then ask individual students what their own ideas were compared with what the article says.

Answers

a He is eating rubbish: plastic cups, paper plates, newspapers, aluminium foil, old milk cartons, aluminium cans, old batteries and glass.

b No, people do not usually eat these things.

c He is trying to make the country cleaner.

d He finds them in dustbins.

e His family and friends think he is crazy.

f His neighbours no longer trust him / don't like him and avoid him.

Look!

- Students look at the different words in British English and American English and compare them.

Exercise 3

- Students find the expressions in the article and write the answers to the questions.

Answers

a Frank did not pay any money. The 'price' he paid was the loss of his wife and many of his friends.

b 'We' are everybody, or people in general. We know this because Frank is not with anyone else at the moment.

c Frank is not talking about the sea. He does not think he is making a big difference.

Exercise 4

- Organize students into groups of four to six if you have a large class, or pairs in a small class. Read out the questions and allow students a few minutes to discuss each one.

- Ask each group to choose a spokesperson to feed back their ideas to the class. Open the discussion out into a whole class discussion.

Exercise 5

- Put students into groups and ask them to design an environmental poster. Make sure that they discuss what they want to say and write out a draft of their text for correction. Ask them also to plan a design together. Encourage them to include illustrations and to create a bold design for maximum impact.

- Hand out large sheets of paper (A3 if possible) when groups are ready. The finished posters can be displayed on the classroom walls.

Think about it

(Student's Book page 47)

These sections are a basic round-up of the language taught in the unit. They can be done individually or in pairs in class, or for homework, then checked in the next lesson.

Answers

1 b wooden c woollen d metal

2 b wood c wool d metal

3 Students' own answers

4 Students' own answers

Workbook answers

1

paper bag, 9

ivory chopsticks, 2

aluminium can, 1

plastic container, 6

woollen jumper, 4

leather shoe, 5

glass bottle, 7

wooden table, 8

2 Students' own answers

3 Students' own answers

4

2 ✓ He's recycling paper.

3 ✓ She's cycling.

4 ✗ He's wasting electricity.

5 ✓ She's making cloths with her old clothes.

6 ✗ He's wasting water.

5

2 He should use recycled paper.

3 He should turn off the lights when he doesn't need them.

4 He should have showers instead of baths.

5 He shouldn't throw paper away.

6 He should re-use plastic bags.

7 He shouldn't clean his house with strong chemicals.

8 He shouldn't leave the tap running when he brushes his teeth.

6

2 If he uses recycled paper, he'll save trees. / If he doesn't use recycled paper, he'll damage the environment.

3 If he doesn't turn off the lights when he doesn't need them, he'll waste energy. / If he turns off the lights when he doesn't need them, he'll protect the environment.

4 If he has showers instead of baths, he'll save water. / If he doesn't have showers instead of baths, he'll damage the environment.

5 If he throws paper away, he'll damage the environment. / If he doesn't throw paper away, he'll help the environment.

6 If he re-uses plastic bags, he'll protect the environment. / If he doesn't re-use plastic bags, he'll damage the environment.

7 If he cleans his house with strong chemicals, he'll pollute the water. / If he doesn't clean his house with strong chemicals, he'll help the environment.

8 If he doesn't leave the tap running when he brushes his teeth, he'll save water. / If he leaves the tap running when he brushes his teeth, he'll damage the environment.

7

2 should	**5** should	**7** shouldn't
3 shouldn't	**6** shouldn't	**8** should
4 shouldn't		

8 *Students' own answers*

Dictionary skills

1 US

2 United States (of America)

3 *Students' own answers*

9 *Students' own answers*

Buzz words

aluminium	leather
chopsticks	paper
container	plastic
cotton	pollution
environment	recycling
forest	wood
fur	wooden
glass	wool
ivory	woollen

Revision

Stop and think!

The exercises and activities in this unit revise all the language taught in Units 6–10. It is divided into five sections. The HELP Screen suggests extra help or activities. Encourage students to refer to these while they are working or set them as homework. When they can do each section, students can colour the letters.

⬤ have to/needn't

(Student's Book page 48)

Exercise 1

- Ask students to describe the picture on page 48. If anyone has worked in a burger bar, ask them to say what it is like, or elicit students' ideas with a few questions, for example, *What do you have to do? You have to serve food.*

- Get students to read through the dialogue and complete it with *have to* or *needn't*. Check concepts: if you *have to* do something you have no choice, if you *needn't* do something, it is not necessary to do it but you can if you want to.

- Students can then role-play the conversation in pairs. Go through the answers with whole class.

Answers

have to   needn't   have to   have to   have to
needn't

⬤ Routines

(Student's Book page 49)

Exercise 1

- Revise adverbs of frequency with the whole class by looking at the diagram in the picture on page 49. Ask students *Do you eat breakfast?* Get them to put up their hands in response to your prompts: *always? usually?* etc. Go through the other adverbs to check everyone understands which number represents which adverb.

- Ask students to look at the information in the table about John and Carol and focus on the example sentence, John *nearly always has a shower before breakfast.* In pairs, they use the chart to make up more sentences about John and Carol using the chart, for example, *Carol hardly ever has a shower*

before breakfast, John rarely misses lunch. Make sure the third person singular form of the verb is used and point out that the main stress is usually on the adverb. Then ask them to write sentences 1–5.

Answers

1   Carol occasionally misses lunch.
2   Carol sometimes does her homework in class.
3   John often pretends to be ill on schooldays.
4   John always goes to bed before midnight.
5   Carol never pretends to be ill on schooldays.

- Students fill in column 3 in the table and then ask their partner questions with *How often …?* to fill in column 4.

- With the whole class, ask students to respond to questions about the table. Make sure that they use the right verb form for the third person, and that they put the adverb of frequency before the verb. For example:

How often does Maria go to bed before midnight? She nearly always goes to bed before midnight.

Exercise 3

- Tell students to write true sentences in their notebooks using adverbs from the list. Encourage them to write about different activities from the ones in the table. Give a few suggestions, for example, *I always help with the housework, Peter often goes swimming.*

⬤ Present simple/continuous

(Student's Book page 49)

Exercise 1

- Ask students to look at the pictures from Susan's video and to talk about what is happening in them, using the present continuous. For example:

The family are in the kitchen having breakfast.
Susan and her friends are waiting for the bus.
The kids on the bus are making a noise.
Susan is sitting in her classroom.

- Ask students to read the text and fill in the gaps using the correct form of the verbs in brackets.

Answers

1 are having 2 have 3 is smiling
4 am filming 5 don't talk 6 catch
7 is arriving 8 go 9 is wearing 10 wears
11 am sitting 12 arrives 13 is shouting
14 is telling 15 behave 16 don't know
17 sit 18 comes 19 is making 20 have to

● Present simple passive

(Student's Book page 50)

Exercise 1

- Pre-teach vocabulary that is likely to be unfamiliar (e.g. *episode, decorate, fabric*). Tell students to choose words/phrases from each column in the box to make sentences. Read the example with the whole class and ask students to write the other sentences in their notebooks.

Exercise 2

- Write the example sentences in the active and passive on the board:

  Carole makes the models. The models are made by Carole.

- Revise how the present passive is formed.

- Get students to change sentences 1–5 from active to passive in the same way. They can do it orally in pairs first, then write the sentences. Go around and check the answers individually or elicit correct answers with the whole class and write them on the board.

Answers

1 Our homework is corrected by the teacher.
2 All our meals are cooked by Dad.
3 The class newspaper is designed by Samantha.
4 The photos are taken by Terry.
5 The spelling is checked by the editor.

● Past continuous

(Student's Book page 50)

Exercise 1

- Ask students what a car crash is. If anyone has been in a crash, let them tell the class about it.

- Focus students' attention on the picture on page 50 for a couple of minutes, then ask them to close their books. Tell them that this car crash happened yesterday and ask them to remember all they can about the picture of this event. In pairs, they discuss what happened and what people were doing when the car crashed. After a few minutes, they can open their books and check the details together.

- Now ask students to answer questions 1–4. Give them time to write the answers down, then go through them with whole class.

Answers

1 He was watching TV.
2 Sara was working on the computer.
3 She was feeding chickens.
4 No he wasn't, he was reading a book.

Exercise 2

- Write on the board: *the twins/sunbathe?* and elicit the question *Were the twins sunbathing?* Refer students to the picture and elicit the answer: *No they weren't. They were playing basketball.*

- Give the prompts for questions 1–4 and elicit questions and answers in the same way. Ask students to write them in their notebooks.

Answers

1 Were Mrs Collins and Mrs King eating? No they weren't. They were drinking tea.
2 Was Uncle Ben mending his car? No he wasn't. He was washing his bicycle.
3 Was Simon having a bath? No he wasn't. He was having a shower.
4 Was the dog eating? No it wasn't. It was sleeping.

● Reading and writing

(Student's Book page 51)

Exercise 1

- Look at the picture and elicit *They are playing chess*. If possible, find a student who plays chess and get him/her to tell the class something about the game (where and when he/she plays, who with, how long the game takes, etc.).

- Ask students to read the text. Encourage them to ask or use a dictionary if there are any words they do not know.

Exercise 2

- Students read the sentences 1–5 and decide if they are true or false.

Answers

1 false 2 false 3 true 4 true 5 false

Exercises 3 and 4

- Ask students to make notes about their own hobby, using the prompts given and adding any other information they choose. While they are making notes, circulate and help with ideas and vocabulary.

• Students then write a description of their hobby.

Project idea
(Student's Book page 51)

Organize the class into groups of students who share the same hobbies or are interested in the same sports. Ask them to find out all they can about their hobby/sport. As well as the ideas in the Student's Book, you could suggest that they find out about:

– famous people who have been involved with their hobby/sport
– information about competitions or exhibitions
– names and addresses of clubs
– places where you can find equipment or materials needed.

• The finished charts can be displayed in the classroom.

Dear Sue ...

Learning objectives

- describing emotions
- describing problems
- giving advice

Language focus

- present simple with descriptive adjectives
- *If I were you, I'd ...* for advice

Active vocabulary

confident	depressed	embarrassed
excited	insecure	jealous
moody	negative	nervous
optimistic	pessimistic	popular
positive	self-conscious	shy
worried		

Receptive vocabulary

advice	anxious	ashamed
attention	bored	compliment
copy (*verb*)	exactly	faint (*verb*)
friendly	guilty	haircut
hopeful	ignore	invent
miserable	obvious	overworked
phobia	phone-in	pocket money
relax	respect (*verb*)	scared
self-confidence	spider	take notice of
tell a lie	temporary	twin
ugly	unfair	unfriendly
unpleasant		

Materials

Problem pages from magazines for Lead-in b.

Copies of photocopiable page 11 for Additional activity 2.

Lead-ins

a   Revise what things are made of. Write *cotton*, *paper*, *plastic*, *wood*, *leather*, *glass* on the board. Give students two minutes to write down as many things as they can think of which are made from these materials.

b   Show students some magazines. Ask them if they ever read problem pages. Ask what kind of problems people write about.

Tell students that they are going to visit an 'agony aunt'. Get them to write down two or three problems that they can ask about.

c   Tell students how you feel today, for example, *I'm happy because the weather is good*. Ask how individual students are feeling. Try to elicit a variety of adjectives.

Vocabulary

(Student's Book page 52)

Exercise 1

• Ask students to look at the photos and answer the questions.

Exercise 2

• Students read the letter. They should now be able to identify Joanna and Natalie in the photos.

• Ask students if they have ever experienced a similar problem to Natalie's.

Exercise 3

• a: Students read through the list of adjectives, checking in the glossary for any they don't know or recognize.

• b: Ask them to find words in the list which describe the people in the photos in Exercise 1. In pairs or groups, students compare and discuss their answers.

• You could ask some pairs/groups to read out their answers and ask if the rest of the class think that there are definite correct answers and definite wrong answers.

Answers

Answers here will be subjective, depending on students' interpretation. While Natalie is apparently *popular* and *confident* in the first picture, she is also *worried* and *embarrassed* by the situation with Joanna. Joanna looks *depressed* in the last picture. She may be *nervous* and *insecure*, and other adjectives in the list may also be appropriate.

• c: Students look at the list again and decide which adjectives are positive and which are negative. Go through the examples in the diagrams with them first.

Answers

Positive: popular   optimistic   excited   confident

Negative: nervous   pessimistic   moody   worried   jealous   embarrassed   insecure   self-conscious   depressed

Exercise 4

• Read through the list of situations with the students and give them a few minutes to think about them.

• In pairs or groups, students talk about their feelings in each of these situations.

Additional activity 1

Get students to pair the adjectives with their opposites where possible, for example, *happy/sad*, *confident/shy* or *worried*, *optimistic/pessimistic*. Ask them to make a list of opposites for the adjectives in Exercise 3.

Additional activity 2

Pairwork: Make enough copies of photocopiable page 11 for each pair, and cut them into parts A and B. Tell students that Vasilis and Christina have written to a magazine 'agony aunt' called Sue, but their letters have got mixed up. Ask students to take it in turns to read out a sentence from their sheet and decide together whose letter it belongs to. When they have sorted out the two letters, ask pairs to discuss what advice Sue should give in each case.

Language focus

(Student's Book page 53)

Exercise 1 🎞️ **①**

• Ask students if they ever listen to the radio and if they have ever written to a radio programme or been on a radio programme.

• Explain that they are now going to listen to the first part of a radio programme for teenagers. Natalie (from Vocabulary Exercises 2 and 3) has sent her letter to this programme.

• Students listen to item 1 and say what Sue Wallace does (she is a counsellor who specializes in teenage problems).

🎞️ **TAPESCRIPT**

DJ ... and you're listening to Best FM – music to your ears 24 hours a day. You're never alone. I'm Jack Powell, with you until midnight, playing your favourite pop and rock. Lots of music to come, but right now it's time for Close Call, our regular phone-in spot. And with us in the studio is Sue Wallace, who as you know is a counsellor specializing in teenage problems. As usual, she's going to offer her advice on *your* problems. Just pick up the phone and dial 01865 277227 and tell us your problem. If you don't want to phone, you can write to us at Jack Powell's Chart Show, Best FM, Oxford OX2 6DP, and Sue will help you. Here's our first letter, and it's from a girl called Natalie. She writes: 'Joanna, a girl in my class, copies everything I do. Last week, I had a haircut, so she went and had exactly the same haircut the next day. Two days ago, I went to school wearing a new T-shirt. Two days later, she came to school wearing an identical T-shirt. It's really beginning to annoy me. Everyone at school calls us "the twins". My mum says she is probably jealous of me, but I don't know what to do about it. Please can you help me? Yours, Natalie'.

Exercise 2

- In pairs or groups, students think of advice they would give to Natalie. Check that they are using *should* and *shouldn't* for advice when writing down their ideas.

Exercise 3 📟 ❷

- Students listen to item 2 and compare Sue's advice to Natalie with theirs. Ask them if their advice was the same or different. Which advice do they think is best? Discuss this with the whole class.

📟 TAPESCRIPT

DJ '… My mum says she is probably jealous of me, but I don't know what to do about it. Please can you help me? Yours, Natalie.' Sue, over to you. What would you do in Natalie's situation? Any ideas?

Sue Well, the problem's not really that unusual. Teenagers often copy one another. But Natalie – I hope you're listening, Natalie – I can understand why you feel unhappy about it, but I can also see that in some ways, it's a great compliment to you. Joanna obviously copies you because she thinks you look great! Anyway, if I were you, I would thank her for the compliment. Then maybe I'd suggest that a different colour would look better on her. Look, Natalie, I'm sure it's just a temporary situation – she'll stop copying you soon. If I were you, I wouldn't worry about it too much.

Exercise 4

- Students listen to Sue again and complete the text in their books.
- Play the tape again to allow students to check their answers, pausing as necessary.

Answers

1 thank 2 suggest 3 worry

Focus

- Explain that this is an expression we use to give advice. Point out that you always say *If I were you*, not *If I was you*.
- Students look back at the text they completed in Exercise 4 and find examples of this form of advice (*If I were you, I would thank … If I were you, I wouldn't worry …*).
- Check understanding of the form and usage by asking questions a and b.

Answers

a I'd

b she is imagining herself in Natalie's position.

- Read through the examples of other ways to give advice before students begin their role-plays in Exercise 6.

Exercise 5

- Students read John's letter and answer the questions in their notebooks.

Answers

a He is worried about the change in his best friend's behaviour.

b What's your advice? What do you think I should do?

Exercise 6

- Put the class into pairs. In each pair, Student A is Jack Powell and Student B is Sue Wallace. Ask them to role-play the radio dialogue using John's letter from Exercise 5.
- Remind B students that they can use their notes from Exercise 5c to help them give John advice.
- When they have finished, ask some pairs to come to the front of the class and act out their dialogue. Find out if the class agrees on the advice that they should give John.

Exercise 7

- In different pairs, students read through the list of situations on page 53. Ask them to discuss the four problems (or they can substitute different problems of their own), taking it in turns to ask for and give advice.
- When they have finished ask the class to exchange ideas and discuss the best advice to give for each problem.

Go back to the list of problems students wrote for the 'agony aunt' in Lead-in b. Divide the class into two groups, A and B. Members of Group A take it in turns to read out their problems. Group B are the agony aunts who give advice using *If I were you …* or one of the other expressions from the Focus box. They can then change roles, with B reading the problems and A giving advice.

Skills focus

(Student's Book page 54)

Exercise 1

- Students look at the letters and the headings on page 30. Give them a few minutes to think what problem each letter might be about and elicit some suggestions.

Exercise 2

- Give students a time limit of three or four minutes to read the three letters. They should not worry about the meaning of every word – they only need to skim-read to find the answers. However, help them with the words *spider* and *panic attack* if necessary.

Answers

b Letter 3 is about not having control over a situation.

Letter 1 is about self-confidence.

Letter 2 is about fears.

▶ **Note**

Point out that *to be scared of, to be afraid of* and *to have a fear of* something all mean the same. However, when people say *I'm afraid*, it can also mean *I am sorry*, for example *I'm afraid you can't go out tonight.*

Exercise 3

- In pairs, students read the letters again and make notes in the table for each heading. They can then compare answers in groups.

Exercise 4

- Students read two replies to Letter 2 ('Spider terror') and choose which is the better reply. Ask them to discuss their choice with the rest of the class and try to come to a general consensus.

- If students have selected reply a as the most appropriate, explain that reply b shows a better understanding of the problem and makes the writer feel more confident that he/she is not alone. Ask students to find the phrases in reply b which show this (*I don't think you're being silly, Phobias are very serious, If I were you*).

Exercise 5

- Students choose one of the other two letters and write advice to the writer.

- Make sure that they plan their replies beforehand and consult the Focus box on page 53 for useful expressions to use.

- Students read out their replies to the class. Find out what the rest of the class think about their advice. They can agree or disagree using the phrases *I agree. I think that's good advice.* or *I don't agree. I don't think he/she should do that.* As a class, students can decide on the best advice for each letter.

Ask students if they know of other phobias, e.g. fear of heights, fear of falling, fear of small spaces. Tell them you have a phobia, for example, you are scared of flying. What advice can they give? Now ask if any of the students are afraid of anything. What advice can other students give to them?

Think about it!

(Student's Book page 55)

These sections are a basic round-up of the language taught in the unit. They can be done individually or in pairs in class, or for homework, then checked in the next lesson.

Answers

1 **b** embarrassed   **c** depressed   **d** excited

2 *Students' own answers*

3 *(Possible answers)*

   b Why don't you write a letter to him?

   c How about buying a new bike?

   d If I were you, I wouldn't buy that CD.

   e I think you shouldn't go.

Workbook answers

❶

1 He's going to be told off. He's worried and nervous. / He looks worried.

2 She's leaning against a wall and chatting with her friends. She's popular and confident. / She looks popular and confident.

3 He's sitting alone in the classroom. He's thinking about his next lesson. He looks depressed and pessimistic.

4 She's standing in the corner, away from the other girls. She looks insecure and jealous.

❷ *Students' own answers*

Buzzwords

1	sad	6	moody	10	pessimistic
2	depressed	7	anxious	11	nervous
3	jealous	8	optimistic	12	popular
4	confident	9	excited	13	embarrassed
5	insecure				

The hidden word is *self-conscious*.

Definition: nervous or shy because you are worried about what other people think of you

❸

2	were	9	would want
3	would sit down	10	will phone
4	talk	11	won't have
5	would try	12	won't eat
6	would say	13	will keep
7	would spend	14	won't watch
8	were		

❹

1 14

2 her younger brother

3 He goes into her room whenever he feels like it. He won't let her study, speak to her friends, listen to music, or even rest, without disturbing her.

4 She loves him, but his behaviour is making her desperate.

5 She doesn't want to upset him. Once, when she threw him out of her room, he cried for hours.

❺

If I were you, I would sit down and talk to him. I would try to see (everything from) his point of view. I would explain why you need some time to yourself, and promise to play with him for a while in the afternoon. If I were you, I would talk to your parents. I would ask them to help, and give your brother things to do …

Students' own answers

❻

1 If I were you, I'd go to the first party until about nine o'clock and then explain to your best friend why you have to leave so early. Then go to the second party.

2 If I were you, I'd go to Britain for a month. But you can still start saving up for a computer.

3 If I were you, I'd buy the two T-shirts and the jeans, and start saving up for the jacket.

❼

2 I wouldn't touch the light with wet hands. You'll get an electric shock.

3 I wouldn't light a fire there. You'll start a fire!

4 I wouldn't dive there. You'll have a bad accident.

5 I wouldn't cycle to school in the rush-hour. You'll get knocked off.

6 I wouldn't do that! The tiger will bite you!

❽

(Possible answers)

2 Why don't you take the bus?

3 How about buying some new clothes?

4 I think you should talk to her about it.

5 Why don't you ask the doctor for some advice?

6 I don't think you should break the window! Why don't you ask the neighbours if they have a spare key?

Dictionary skills

1	2	2	2	3	2

Can you believe it?

Learning objectives

- agreeing and disagreeing with degrees of certainty
- talking about the past
- describing experiences and achievements

Language focus

- modals *can/can't/could/must be* to express certainty
- present perfect

Active vocabulary

believe	bungee-jumping	contract (*noun*)
film studio	hit record	hot-air balloon
luxury	marry	millionaire
set a record	sign	yet

Receptive vocabulary

achievement	amazing	astronaut
couple	dialogue	disbelief
experience	experiment	fact
fashion model	golden	imaginary
key word	liquid (*noun*)	Mars
mountaineer	novel (*noun*)	orbit (*verb*)
population	presenter	publish
space	succeed	university degree
Venus		

Materials

A photo of a famous, wealthy film star for Lead-in b.

Copies of photocopiable page 12 for Additional activity 3.

Lead-ins

a   Students tell you about past holidays. Ask students where they went and when they went there. You could write each place and date in a corner of the blackboard.

b   Hold up a photo of a famous, wealthy film star. Ask students where they think this person goes on his/her holidays. What else does the person do with his/her money, do they think?

Vocabulary

(Student's Book page 56)

Exercise 1

- To set ideas going on these questions about belief and disbelief, tell one or two stories yourself, if possible, about strange or unlikely events in your own experience, or which you have heard or read about. Then ask students to contribute their own stories.

Exercise 2 📼 ❶

- a: Get students to read the list of expressions in their books. In pairs or groups, they put these expressions into three different categories.

Answers

You believe someone: It must be true. It sounds OK to me. Yes, I believe that.

You don't believe someone: It can't be true. You're having me on. I don't believe that. No, that's impossible. You're making it up.

You aren't sure: It could be true. It sounds possible.

- b and c: Ask students if they think all the expressions in the second category are the same. Do they think some are stronger than others? Allow a few minutes' discussion and then ask for feedback.
- Play item 1. Students check their answers.

Exercise 3

- Focus on the pictures around the text first. Get students to describe each one. Put any key words on the board.

Additional activity 1

Focus on the picture of the baby wearing the crown. Ask students to tell you what they think is happening (the baby has become king at eight months old). Do they believe that this is possible? Get them to use appropriate phrases from their lists in Exercise 2 to give their opinions.

- Read the eight 'facts' as a class. Have a brief discussion about similar stories that the students know.
- Now give students a time limit to read the stories and to decide if they think all the 'facts' are true. Remind them that they do not have to understand every word of the texts, but help with any unknown vocabulary where necessary.

Exercise 4

- a: In pairs, students say what they think of the 'facts'. Encourage them to use as many phrases as possible from the list of expressions in Exercise 2.
- b: Students make notes of their decisions with ticks if they believe the 'facts', crosses if they don't believe them and question marks if they are not sure.
- c: In larger groups, students discuss their opinions. Does everyone agree?
- Now tell them which stories are really true. Are they surprised?

Answers

Facts b, d and h are false.

Language focus

(Student's Book page 57)

Exercise 1

- Focus on the photograph. Get the class to tell you all they can about the people they can see.

Exercise 2

- Read the instructions and questions a, b and c. Now get students to read the passage to find the answers.

Answers

a He became rich when he set up his own computer games company.

b He says he has done everything, he has been everywhere and he has lived life to the full.

c He has been to America, his favourite continent.
He speaks Norwegian and he likes it best.
He has married one of the most beautiful girls in the world, top fashion model Fay Waif.

Focus

- Read through the Focus notes and the example sentences.
- Now refer back to the information you put on the board in Lead-in a, about students' holidays. Use these as a model to talk about the students' experiences, for example: *You have been to Kos. You haven't been to Italy. He's been to Istanbul.*
- Point out that the present perfect is being used here to talk about life up to now, not about a specific event.
- Point out that all forms of the verb take *have* or *'ve*, except *he* or *she* which take *has* or *'s*. The past participle is often the same as the past simple form, but not always: tell students they must learn the ones that are irregular.

Have a class drill. Say the following: *I've lived life to the full.* Students repeat.

Now say *he.* Students say *He's lived life to the full.* Do the same with *she, you, we.*

Now change the sentence slightly. Say *London, I've lived in London.* Students repeat.

Now say a verb, for example, *work.* Students say *I've worked in (place).*

Give further word prompts for students to change the sentence each time, for example: *I've worked in a restaurant. I've bought a restaurant. She's bought a house. She's bought a computer.*

Exercise 3

- Students make the sentence in pairs or individually from the prompts provided. Go round and monitor their work to check they are not making mistakes. Encourage pairs of students to help each other with the sentences.

Answers

a He's set the world record for bungee-jumping.

b He's bought luxury houses in Hawaii, Thailand and the South of France.

c He's crossed the Atlantic Ocean in a hot-air balloon.

d He's made a hit record.

e He's signed a contract with Warner Brothers film studios.

Exercise 4

- In pairs, students write unbelievable achievements for Marcus. See which pair can come up with the most ridiculous claim!

- Go over their answers with the class, and put a few on the board.

Exercise 5

- a: In pairs, students discuss things they have done in their lives and make notes.

- Go through the example with them before they begin and remind them of the present perfect construction which they should use in their discussion.

- b: In the same pairs students now discuss and make notes about the things they haven't done in their lives but would like to do.

- Go through the example with them before they begin and point out the present perfect negative form and the expression *I'd like to.*

Pairwork: make enough copies of photocopiable page 12 for each pair, and cut them into parts A and B. Student A has to use the prompts to make present perfect questions about Jason, and Student B about Kylie. They reply with *Yes he/she has* or *No, he/she hasn't* by referring to the pictures in their photo album. Encourage them to add extra details in their replies.

Skills focus

(Student's Book page 58)

Exercise 1

- Students look at the pictures and answer the questions. Go through the list of names beforehand to make sure they know which are male and which are female names. You may want to introduce the expression *chat show* to describe this type of TV programme.

Answers

Ben Yates 5   Fay Waif 4   Marcus Samson 2
Molly Jones 3   Rachel Krantz 1

Exercise 2

- a: Read the instructions and the list of words. Go through the example with the students, pointing out the meaning of *already* and its position in the sentence.

- Students now use the present perfect to make a list of everything Marcus says he has done.

- b: Students look back at page 57 (the article and the list in Exercise 3) to check the lists they have made. Ask some students to read out some of the items on their lists at this point.

- c: Ask students what they think of Marcus – do they believe that he has done all of these things? Does everyone agree about what they think he has and hasn't done?

Exercise 3 📼 ❷

- Tell students that they are going to hear part of the TV chat show about Marcus. Ask them to listen to what the three people say about him and put either a tick or a cross beside each achievement in their list.

- This dialogue is long, with quite a lot of detail. Make sure students realize that they are not expected to understand every word. Draw their attention to the listening tip and go over the list of words in Exercise 2a – these are key words which they can expect to hear and which will help them to focus on the information they need.

- Play item 2. Ask students to compare answers in pairs, and then play the item again, with pairs again comparing notes at the end. Replay the item once more so that they can check their answers.

TAPESCRIPT

Rachel The next item on our show concerns a report in the *Daily Clarion* newspaper two weeks ago, on a certain Marcus Samson, described as 'Golden Boy Marcus'. According to the report, Marcus Samson has done it all – he's been everywhere, seen everything, and has got everything a young man could want – and he's still only 18. An amazing story. Good luck to him, you might think. But the day after the report appeared in the newspaper, *Life's Like That* received a call from Ben Yates, Marcus's old school friend. Apparently, Marcus Sampson isn't his real name at all. His real name is Mark Smith. This is what Ben has to say.

Ben Well, I was amazed when I read the story, it's all a pack of lies. We grew up together and went to school together. What's all this about travel? He's never been outside England. The furthest he's ever been is the seaside, in Blackpool! And he never did his French homework, and can't speak any language except English. He certainly hasn't bought any luxury houses – not in Thailand, Hawaii, or anywhere else! No, I think he's doing all this just to get attention – he wants people to think well of him. So he's invented all these stories. He says he's made a hit record, and signed a contract with Warner Brothers film studios – it's just not true. He's made it all up. What an idiot!

Rachel Interesting, isn't it? We thought it was worth finding out more, so we went up to Manchester and we found one of Marcus's – sorry, Mark's – neighbours, Mrs Molly Jones. Molly's with us in the studio now. Molly, what do you know about this boy?

Molly Mark's always been one for telling stories, you know, but this one's a whopper. I liked the bit about bungee-jumping – he's never done any bungee-jumping in his life. He's scared stiff of heights. He can't even go to the top of the stairs without feeling sick. And he says he's crossed the Atlantic in a hot-air balloon? The only balloon he's ever had was a Mickey Mouse balloon from the fair when he was a boy. He's telling fibs, you know.

Rachel Well, that comes from people who know him well. What about his millions in the bank? Is he really a millionaire? Hear what Roger Tumtree, his bank manager, told us.

Roger 2.7 million? There are too many zeros, I'm afraid. He has exactly twenty-seven pounds in his account. He's never been very rich, and I don't think he ever will be.

Rachel And what about all these famous people? Models, film stars, pop stars. We've got model Fay Waif in the studio. Fay – you're Marcus Samson's wife, aren't you?

Fay Marcus Samson? Who's he? I've never heard of him

Rachel So there you have it – Marcus Samson, or rather, Mark Smith – a remarkable 18-year-old with a remarkable talent … for telling lies. Maybe he has done all these things – in his dreams. If you're watching, Marcus, we'd advise you to … grow up, and don't tell lies – sooner or later you'll get found out.

Exercise 4

- In pairs or groups, students talk about the things Marcus has and hasn't done. Go through the example, first focusing particularly on the negative form of the present perfect in the first example.

Suggested answers

He hasn't travelled. He's never been outside England.

He hasn't bought any luxury houses.

He hasn't made a hit record. He's made it all up.

He's never done any bungee-jumping in his life.

He hasn't crossed the Atlantic in a balloon.

He hasn't married a model.

He has made up all these stories.

Exercise 5

- Students look at this picture from another part of the TV show. Ask them what is happening (Rachel Krantz is interviewing a different man) and to predict what this man says has happened. Use this as an opportunity to pre-teach *spaceship*, *alien* and *abduct* before students listen to the cassette.

Exercise 6 ▣ ❸

- Play item 3. Students listen and check their answers to Exercise 5.
- Play the cassette again. Students tick the things that Mike says have happened to him.

Answers

b ✓ e ✓ f ✓ i ✓

🎙 TAPESCRIPT

Rachel And now, our final feature for today's programme. Meet Mike Dix. Hello Mike.

Mike Hi, Rachel.

Rachel Now, Mike. You say that you've had some strange experiences over the past few months, don't you?

Mike Yes, that's right. I …

Rachel Let me stop you there, Mike. Because before we talk about it, I want the viewers to watch this reconstruction …

Voice The time – December 11th 1995. The place – a deserted road 25 miles from the nearest town.

Jenny Hello, can I help you?. You must be freezing. Can I take you some place?

Mike Th-Thanks. I've lost my coat and shoes … and it's a long walk in this cold. Can you take me to Glenwood?

Jenny Sure, no problem. It's on my route. But what's happened? Why are you here, in the middle of nowhere, with no coat or shoes?

Mike You won't believe me if I tell you. In fact, I can hardly believe it myself. I've … I've been abducted.

Jenny Abducted? But why? Are you someone important?

Mike What date is it?

Jenny December 11th.

Mike It can't be … unless I've travelled back in time.

Jenny Travelled back in time? What are you talking about?

Mike Well, I left on December 12th and now you say it's the eleventh … Unless … What year is it?

Jenny 1995 of course.

Mike What! Then I've been away a year! I've been on that spaceship for a year!

Jenny Spaceship? This is crazy. Who are you, anyway?

Mike My name's Mike Dix and I'm …

Jenny Oh, I get it. You're the guy who disappeared. Look, why don't you start at the beginning and tell me what happened?

Mike Well, I was driving along near here when I saw a bright light. I couldn't see properly, so I stopped the car. Then suddenly the light shone on me and sort of sucked me into the spaceship. Since that time I've been a scientific experiment.

Jenny What do you mean?

Mike Well, they kind of did tests on me. I guess it was to find out what humans are like. I've eaten food and drunk liquids that don't exist on Earth. I've looked in a mirror and seen right through my body, like an X-ray, and I've talked in a language from another planet. I've visited Mars and Venus. Oh, and I've seen people who are dead, like Albert Einstein … and before you ask, no, I haven't seen Elvis Presley!

Jenny You seem to have had an exciting time, but I don't believe a word of it. So where have you really been for a year?

Mike I told you. I've been in a spaceship!

Rachel So, there you have it. Mike Dix – abducted by aliens. But is his story true?

Exercise 7

- In pairs, students correct the sentences. Play the cassette again if necessary.

Answers

a He's lost his coat and shoes.
c He's seen Albert Einstein.
d He hasn't travelled back in time. (He's been away for a year).
g He's eaten food that doesn't exist on Earth.
h He's talked in a language from another planet.

▶ **Note**
Point out that this exercise uses irregular past participles: *seen* (*to see*) and *eaten* (*to eat*).

Exercise 8

- Have a brief class discussion about whether the students believe Mike's story or not. Encourage them to use expressions from the list in Vocabulary Exercise 2.

Exercise 9

- Give the students five minutes to write down one true and one imaginary experience. Ask them not to discuss these with anybody else.
- Divide the class into groups of three or four students and ask them to take it in turn to read out their two descriptions, in either order. The others have to guess which experience is the true one.

Write the following on the board. Students must tell you which ones they believe, using language from the unit (the answers are given in brackets).

1   The Greek football team has only been in one World Cup. (true)
2   Sicily is further south than Crete. (false)
3   Gambia in Africa is in the same time zone as England. (true)
4   95% of the human body is water. (true)
5   More people speak English in the world than any other language (false – more people speak Chinese).

Think about it!

(Student's Book page 59)

These sections are a basic round-up of the language taught in the unit. They can be done individually or in pairs in class, or for homework, then checked in the next lesson.

Answers

1   (Possible answers)
    I agree. That's right.
    I don't agree. That can't be true

2   Students' own answers

3   Students' own answers

Workbook answers

❶

1 It's possible.	5 It must be true.
2 It must be true.	6 It's possible.
3 It's possible.	7 It must be true.
4 It can't be true.	8 It can't be true.

❷

2   Roald Amundsen didn't invent the telephone in 1876. He was the first person to reach the South Pole on 16 December 1911.

3   Captain James Cook and his men were not the first pop group to sell more than 1,000 million records and cassette tapes. They were the first men to cross the Antarctic Circle in January 1773.

4   Henry Ford didn't discover radium. He built the first petrol-driven car in 1896, and started the Ford Motor Company in 1903.

5   Marie and Pierre Curie didn't build the first petrol-driven car. They discovered radium and won the Nobel Prize for Chemistry in 1911.

6   The Beatles weren't the first men to cross the Antarctic Circle. They were the first pop group to sell more than 1,000 million records and cassette tapes.

❸

3   He has flown in an aeroplane.
4   He hasn't eaten meat.
5   He hasn't made a million.
6   He has been to Paris.
7   He hasn't passed his driving test.
8   He has seen the Niagara Falls.

❹   Students' own answers

❺

1   He is one of Britain's best and most famous snow-boarders.
2   He's from Aberdeen in Scotland.
3   He was the first Scotsman to try snow-boarding in Scotland.
4   Yes, he is successful.

b   He's participated in snow-boarding races in Europe and North America.

c   He's learnt a lot in the last years and he's taught other people who would like to become snow-boarders.

d   He's set up the Hyper Active Snow camps in Scotland to allow young people to learn basic and advanced snow-boarding skills at their own pace.

e   He's taught many young snow-boarders how to 'surf' down the mountain or do difficult tricks on the board.

f   He thinks he's started the snow-boarding revolution in Scotland.

❻   Students' own answers

❼

2 visited	7 loved	12 spoken
3 seen	8 travelled	13 done
4 met	9 ridden	14 cheated
5 been	10 drunk	15 smoked
6 liked	11 eaten	16 broken

❽

2 are	6 have taken
3 have done	7 have entered
4 have studied	8 have heard
5 play	

❾ *Students' own answers*

Buzz words

1 lost
2 met
3 done
4 Across: bought; Down: been
5 made
6 eaten
7 tried
8 had
9 seen
10 become
11 drunk

The secrets of your dreams

Learning objectives

- describing dreams
- talking about general and specific past experiences
- talking about symbols and associations

Language focus

- gerunds
- present perfect compared with past simple

Active vocabulary

corridor	crash (*noun*)	daydream
dream	drown	fall off
flood	frightening	nightmare
pleasant	run away	strange
symbolize	unpleasant	vehicle

Receptive vocabulary

anxiety	associated with	cave
clown	coral	dream image
during	expert	explorer
fail	gardener	hideaway
joy	make up	novelist
octopus	poem	poet
recurring	safe	sea-bed
secret	shade	solve
symbol	wave (*noun*)	

Materials

Copies of photocopiable page 13 for Additional activity 4.

Lead-ins

a Have a chain story. Ask a student where they have been on holiday, for example:

   A: I've been to Rome.

   Show how the next person must continue, reporting this information and adding their own:

   B: Frank has been to Rome. I've been to Madrid. What about you?

   C: Frank has been to Rome and Gina has been to Madrid. I've been to ...

b Write the word *mountain* on the board. In one minute, students write down as many activities as they can think of that are connected with the word. For example: *walking, climbing, hang-gliding, falling, farming, snowing*, etc.

Vocabulary

(Student's Book page 60)

Background

Many psychologists believe that dreams are a window into the subconscious. They believe that dreams reveal people's anxieties and obsessions.

Exercise 1

- First, get students to tell you as much as they can about the pictures. Help them with the word *corridor* if necessary.
- Now give students a few minutes to discuss the pictures and their dreams in pairs.
- Have a class feedback session. If students have had any of the dreams, ask them to describe how they felt. However, don't press anyone to talk about their dreams if they don't want to.

Exercise 2

- Give students a few minutes to study the words and to find them in the pictures. Help them with vocabulary if necessary.
- Give students about five minutes to make sentences like the examples.Then ask them to read out a sentence each.

Additional activity 1

Get students to divide the list in Exercise 2 into 'good' dream words and 'bad' dream words if appropriate, for example *climbing*, *driving* and *flying* could be good dreams, but *crashing*, *drowning* and *running away* are bad dreams.

Exercise 3

- In pairs or groups, students describe the dreams using the words given. Encourage them to begin their sentences with a gerund (*-ing*), such as *Walking down a dark corridor is scary*, *Crashing a car is unpleasant*, etc.

Additional activity 2

Students list as many other things as they can think of which are frightening, strange, pleasant or unpleasant. They should begin their list with gerunds, for example, *Walking alone at night is frightening*.

Exercise 4

- Quickly read the three questions. Can students guess what the answers are?
- Students read the text to find the answers.

Answers

a A mountain symbolizes a problem or difficulty.

b Falling is associated with fear, worry and anxiety.

c Falling off a mountain symbolizes a problem you do not think you can solve.

▶ Note

Point out that *to fear* and *to be afraid* mean the same thing; there is also little difference in meaning between *anxiety* and *worry*.

Exercise 5

- In pairs, students discuss the other dream images in Exercise 2. If you wish, you could write word prompts on the board to help them, for example, *hope*, *love*, *peace*, *death*, *illness*, *wishes*, *problems*.
- Have a class discussion about the possible meaning of the dreams.

Additional activity 3

Have a chain story round the class. Each student gives a line each about a dream, and then begins a sentence which the next student must complete. For example: *I was walking down a corridor. I saw a light and …* As this is a dream, it does not matter if the story is surreal, as long as it is grammatically correct.

Word grammar

Exercises 6 and 7

- The only word which could replace *Falling* in this example is *Water*. The substitution exercise should show students that the *-ing* word is being used as a noun in this type of sentence.

Pairwork: Make enough copies of photocopiable page 13 for each pair, and cut them into parts A and B. Student A has a scrambled set of sentences describing a dream, and Student B has a set of pictures in the correct order. Give them each a few minutes to look at their sheet. Then ask B to describe the events in sequence to A, who identifies the sentences and numbers the boxes in the right order, 1–8.

Language focus

(Student's Book page 61)

Exercise 1

- Look at the title and the pictures. Ask students to predict what they think the article will be about.

- Read through the questions as a class. Explain that a *recurring dream* is the same dream that returns again and again; *chasing* means 'running after' and a *nightmare* is a very unpleasant dream.

- Give students time to read the text and answer the questions.

Answers

a Mandy   **b** Mandy   **c** Kazim

Focus

- These examples focus on the difference between the present perfect and the past simple. The questions and short answers are in the present perfect, but in the following sentence the tense switches to the past simple (*dreamed*, not *have dreamed*). See if students can work out why.

- The answer is that the speaker is now no longer talking about *any* time in the past right up to the present, but about a particular event at a certain time in the past.

Answers

a present perfect   **b** past simple

- Students use the words on the Vocabulary page to ask and answer questions about dreams. Make sure they use the past tense when they refer to specific times. Go through the example question and answer in their book before they begin.

Exercise 2

- Read through the two questions with the class and ask students to offer their own interpretations.

- Play item 1. Students listen and note down what the expert says about Mandy and Kazim's dreams.

- Play the cassette again, pausing at key points for students to check their answers.

Answers

Mandy's dream: Being chased symbolizes anxiety and the long corridor symbolizes a difficult situation. However, the light at the end of the corridor indicates hope.

Kazim's dream: Flying symbolizes breathing and being alive. The problem during the flight means anxiety about the future.

TAPESCRIPT

We all have dreams, although some people say they do not. This means that they do not remember their dreams, not that they haven't dreamed. The dreams we have when we are sleeping tell us about our lives when we are awake. One of the commonest dreams is the dream of flying. Flying symbolizes breathing, or being alive, so if you enjoyed the flight, it means you are well and happy. However, if there's a problem with the flight – for example, a plane crash – that means you are worried about the future. Another kind of dream which maybe symbolizes anxiety is the dream of being chased. Sometimes people dream that someone is chasing them down a long corridor. This normally means that they are in a difficult situation in their lives. However, if in their dream there is light at the end of the corridor, it means they are basically hopeful about the future.

Exercise 3

- Students listen to item 2 and decide what the expert says about fire, climbing and water. Play the cassette again for students to check their answers.

TAPESCRIPT

Other common dream symbols are fire, climbing, and water. Fire is a strong force in a dream, and so it symbolises your physical and emotional strength. If you cannot put out the fire in your dream and it is destroying everything, it may mean that you are destroying your own life. If you can put out the fire, it means you have control of your emotions. Climbing is associated with ambition. You want to be best at something, pass a test, be the most popular person. If the climb is an easy one, it means you will get what you want. If it is a hard climb, it means you have to work hard to get what you want. All water is associated with the emotions, and the sea symbolises your relationship with your mother. If you are calmly swimming it means you have a good relationship with your mother.

Answers

Refer to the Tapescript above.

Exercise 4

- In pairs, students describe their dreams. They can refer to the vocabulary on the Vocabulary page, but encourage them to use different words if they want to. Help them with any new words.

▶ **Note**

Dreams are very personal and can involve strong emotions. It is probably best to keep these pair discussions private rather than asking for disclosures in front of the whole class that might be embarrassing to individual students.

○ Skills focus

(Student's Book page 62)

Exercise 1

- Look at the titles of the texts and find out what students can predict about them. Help them with other words they are unsure of.
- Students read the texts and discuss the questions in pairs or small groups.

Exercise 2

- Students look at the 'Book of dreams' and read through the questions. At this stage, they don't need to look in detail at the text of the song.

Answers

'Octopus's Garden' is a song about a daydream. The second text (by Susannah York) is about dreams for the future. The third text describes a night-time dream.

Exercise 3

- Students use one of the two outlines to write about their own dreams for the future. First, read through the outlines with the class and elicit suggestions for information that could go in the gaps. Pay particular attention to changes in tense here.

Exercise 4

- Read through the four questions about daydreams with the class and ask a few students to volunteer answers. Make sure they are using *would* when they are imagining an unreal situation in b and c.
- Students make notes based on the questions in their books and then write about their daydreams.

- Monitor the activity, checking that students are using the correct tenses and helping with any vocabulary problems.

Exercise 5 📼 ❸

- Students follow the words for 'Octopus's Garden' while they listen to the song.
- Read the questions in the book and have students volunteer answers.
- Play the cassette again and encourage students to sing along.

📼 **TAPESCRIPT**

Octopus's Garden

I'd like to be under the sea
In an octopus's garden in the shade
He'd let us in, knows where we've been
In his octopus's garden in the shade
I'd ask my friends to come and see
An octopus's garden with me

I'd like to be under the sea
In an octopus's garden in the shade

We would be warm below the storm
In our little hideaway beneath the waves
Resting our head on the sea bed
In an octopus's garden near a cave
We would sing and dance around
Because we know we can't be found

I'd like to be under the sea
In an octopus's garden in the shade

We would shout and swim about
The coral that lies beneath the waves
Oh what joy for every girl and boy
Knowing they're happy and they're safe
We would be so happy, you and me
No one there to tell us what to do

I'd like to be under the sea
In an octopus's garden with you

Exercise 6

- Students use the ideas in the lesson to compile their own 'Book of dreams'.
- Read through the instructions with them as a class, reminding them of the different sorts of texts they can use and about using illustrations and photos.
- Students work in groups to prepare their 'Book of dreams'.

○ Think about it!

(Student's Book page 63)

These sections are a basic round-up of the language taught in the unit. They can be done individually or in pairs in class, or for homework, then checked in the next lesson.

Answers

1 **b** flying **c** driving **d** falling **e** swimming
   f running away

2 **2** f **3** a **4** d **5** b **6** e

3 *Students' own answers*

Workbook answers

❶

2 There's a plane crashing.

3 There's a person driving a truck along a deserted road.

4 There's a person drowning.

5 There's a person falling off a cliff.

6 There's a person flying.

7 There's a person running away.

8 There's a person walking along a long, dark corridor.

9 There's a building being destroyed by a flood.

10 There's a person standing in front of an open door. Beyond the door, there are flowers and a bright light.

❷ *Students' own answers*

Dictionary skills

You can only use the word *anxiety* as a noun. *Anxious* is the adjective. The dictionary definition tells us the parts of speech: *noun* and (the abbreviation) *adj.*

Noun: happiness, confidence
Adjective/modifier: anxious, afraid/fearful, worried, stressful (situation)/'stressed out' (person: colloquial phrase), hopeful, insecure

❸ *Students' own answers*

❹ *Students' own answers*

❺

2 Water symbolizes/is associated with emotions.

3 Climbing symbolizes/is associated with ambition.

4 Light symbolizes/is associated with hope.

5 Being chased symbolizes/is associated with anxiety.

❻

2 stop the van	7 is served
3 find myself	8 is cleared
4 manage to stop	9 go up
5 run towards me	10 get into
6 get out of the van	11 wake up

❼

2 Have you ever climbed a mountain?

3 Have you ever got lost in a strange place?

4 Have you ever met a famous person?

5 Have you ever flown a plane?

6 Have you ever been in a crash?

7 Have you ever been locked out?

8 Have you ever been locked in?

9 Have you ever seen a shark?

10 Have you ever shaken hands with a chimpanzee?

❽ *Students' own answers*

❾

1 wanted	5 remember	9 have changed
2 found	6 sing	10 dreamt/dreamed
3 wrote	7 was	11 have been
4 had	8 wanted	12 wanted

❿ *Students' own answers*

The body beautiful

Learning objectives

- talking about keep-fit activities
- describing how to keep fit
- talking about past habits which are no longer true

Language focus

- *used to* for discontinued habits and activities
- correct stress and intonation in questions

Active vocabulary

accountant	aerobics	cycling
exciting	fast	get the hang of
guy	have a go	instructor
martial arts	relaxing	rock-climbing
rollerblading	slow	snow-boarding
super-fit	used to	weight-training
windsurfing	yoga	

Receptive vocabulary

advert	amazed	audition
colloquial	diet (noun)	exercise
fan	fat	fresh air
gym	keen on	keep-fit activity
mailbox	physically	pretty good
sunshine	unhealthy	

Materials

Photos of people who are famous for what they used to do in the past (e.g. former presidents, sports stars, pop stars, etc.) for Additional activity 3.

Copies of photocopiable page 14 for Additional activity 4.

Lead-ins

a Play 'Keep-fit charades'. Divide the class into four teams. Each team writes down a keep-fit activity. Go round and check that the activities are not the same. Teams take it in turns to select a person from their group to act out the activity to the rest of their group. The rest of the class watches. Give them a time limit of one minute. The team that guesses the activity in the fastest time is the winner.

b Before students open their books, have a brain-storming session. Ask the class to give you as many keep-fit activities as they can think of. Write these on the board.

c Ask students to look at the pictures in the book. Students talk to their partners about which activities they like or are interested in doing (this revises language they met in Unit 1). Have a brief class feedback session.

d Tell students to do certain actions, for example: *Put your hands on your head. Stand up. Comb your hair. Point.* Students must respond by doing the action as fast as possible. The slowest person to do the action each time is out.

Vocabulary

(Student's Book page 64)

Exercise 1

- Students look at the pictures. Read through the questions with them.
- In pairs, students answer the questions.
- Go over their answers as a class.

▶ **Note**

Point out that all the activities listed are noun forms. Except for *martial arts*, they all take a singular verb, including *aerobics*.

Additional activity 1

Students often have problems spelling some of the activities listed. Have a brief class dictation as follows:

I like aerobics. I don't like weight-training. He's interested in climbing and martial arts.

Write the answers on the board and get students to check their partner's work.

Exercise 2

- Students read the three texts about people's favourite ways of keeping fit and answer question a.
- Ask what techniques students used to help them guess the sports. Prompt them by asking, for example, *Why can't 2 be yoga? Why can't 3 be rock-climbing?* Students should be able to identify key words and phrases in each text that help to point to the topic. You might also discuss ways in which the topics can be classified to narrow down the choices (e.g. indoor/outdoor activities, water activities, winter/summer activities).
- Encourage students to look at the words in bold in the text to help them guess which sports are being described.

Answers

1 windsurfing   2 aerobics   3 snow-boarding

Exercise 3

- Play item 1 the cassette for students to listen and check their answers to Exercise 2.

TAPESCRIPT

1

My favourite keep-fit activity is windsurfing. A guy I met on holiday last summer encouraged me to have a go at it. It was difficult at first, but now I'm starting to get the hang of it. And it's much more fun than just sitting around on the beach.

2

I'm really into aerobics. If you like music and you enjoy dancing, it's the perfect way to get fit. But you should start with a class for beginners. Don't pick a class which is only for super-fit people – you won't be able to do it.

3

I love the winter, because it means I can go snow-boarding. I just love the fresh air and the scenery, but the best thing about it is the speed! The first time I tried it, I found it really scary. But as soon as I got to the bottom of the mountain, I couldn't wait to do it again!

Exercise 4

- a: Refer students to the words in bold in the texts in Exercise 2. Explain that all of these words are colloquial expressions.
- Read through the list of more formal expressions 1–9 with the students, and ask them to match expressions from Exercise 2.

Answers

1	very fit	super-fit
2	try it	have a go at it
3	really keen on	really into
4	frightening	scary
5	not doing very much	just sitting around
6	boy (or man)	guy
7	choose	pick
8	immediately wanted to	couldn't wait to
9	be able to do it	get the hang of it

- b: Read the question and the list of possibilities with the students.
- Give them a few minutes to decide when it is a good idea to use colloquial expressions and when it is not a good idea to use them. They tick or cross the appropriate answers.
- Ask for feedback and check they are all aware when colloquial expressions are appropriate.

Answers

You can use colloquial expressions in a letter to your penfriend and when you're talking to your friend.

You shouldn't use colloquial expressions when you are in an exam or talking to an adult you've just met.

Exercise 5

- Give students some time to think about other keep-fit activities they know. Encourage them to use the ones they have already seen in the lesson and to think of some other ones.

- Remind them to use some of the colloquial expressions they have just met.

- Have a class discussion about the activities they know. You can find out the most popular activities and record the results in a graph or chart on the board.

Language focus

(Student's Book page 65)

Exercise 1

- This can be done as a class activity, or you could choose to get students to work in pairs for a few minutes first.

- Students tell you everything they can about the two men. They should use as many descriptive adjectives as they can remember, for example, *fat*, *tired*, *weak*, *healthy*, *fit*. Help them with new words and phrases if necessary, for example *overweight*, *good/bad posture* (how well you hold your body), *glowing with health*.

Exercise 2 📼 ❷

- Play item 2. Students listen to the two men describe themselves and label the pictures.

Answers

Harry: picture 2   Bill: picture 1

📼 TAPESCRIPT

Harry   Hi, I'm Harry. I used to be an accountant and I never took any exercise, so I used to be very unfit. Then one day I looked in the mirror and saw a fat, unhealthy man. I started to go to the gym. Then I discovered windsurfing, so I gave up the gym and spent every weekend windsurfing. I also changed my diet. I used to eat a lot of crisps, chocolate and chips. I didn't use to eat any healthy food at all. Now I eat salads, chicken and fruit. I've changed my job, too. I'm a windsurfing instructor now.

Bill   Hi. My name's Bill. I work in an office. I used to take a lot of exercise – jogging, swimming, football, lots of sport. I was very fit. Then I was made a manager at work. I stopped taking exercise because I worked in the evenings and at weekends. I started living on sandwiches and coffee. I used to eat a much better diet. Now look at me – I'm fat, tired and miserable.

Exercise 3

- Before you play the cassette again, ask students:
  Harry is healthy now. Was he healthy in the past? (No, he wasn't.)
  Bill is unhealthy now. Was he healthy in the past? (Yes, he was.)

- Now write on the board:
  Now Harry is healthy. Harry used to be unhealthy. Now Bill is unhealthy. He used to be healthy.

- Underline the form *used to*, and explain that this form is used to talk about past habits or actions which are not the same now.

- Go through the questions a–h. Now play the cassette and ask students to tick the correct boxes.

Answers

a B **b** H **c** B **d** H **e** H **f** B **g** B **h** H

Focus

- Play the cassette again if necessary. Harry is not an accountant now, he is a windsurfing instructor.

- Read the explanation. Students complete the sentence.

Answer

Harry used to be an accountant, but now he is a windsurfing instructor.

- Give students a few minutes to study the examples in the Focus box. Can they make rules for forming the question and negative form of *used to*?

▶ Note

- Point out the use of *but* to contrast the past and present.

- Make sure students pronounce *used to* correctly (the words run together: /juːstə/). This is different from the verb *use*, for example, *I used a cloth to clean the board* – here *used* is pronounced /juːzd/.

Exercise 4

- Students now use the affirmative and negative forms of *used to* to complete the paragraph about Harry.

Answers

1 used to   **2** used to   **3** didn't use to   **4** used to

▶ Note

Explain that it can be quite rude to call someone *fat*. More polite words to describe fat people include *large* or *plump*.

Additional activity 2

Give students a few minutes to write down as many items of food and drink as they can think of. They then put two headings, *healthy* and *unhealthy*, at the top of another piece of paper.

Students then read their list to a partner, who writes each word under the appropriate heading. At the end of the activity, have a brief class discussion about healthy eating.

Exercise 5

• Students write a paragraph about Bill, using the information from Exercise 3. When they have finished, they can read out their paragraphs to the class.

Exercise 6

• In pairs, students discuss what they used to do. Before they start, tell them a few things you used to do. For example, *I used to sleep in my parents' bed, I used to play with my train set*.

• Students can report back to the class on the things their partner used to do.

Additional activity 3

Hold up photos of people who are famous for things that they used to do (but no longer do), for example John Lennon, Margaret Thatcher, Ben Johnson, Diego Maradona. Get students to tell you about the people with *used to*. For example: *He used to sing with the Beatles. She used to be prime minister of Britain. He used to be a runner. He used to be the best footballer in the world.* Put word prompts on the board to help them if necessary.

Additional activity 4

Pairwork: Make enough copies of photocopiable page 14 for each pair, and cut them into parts A and B. Student A describes Alistair as he *used to be* (e.g. *He used to be fat / have a beard / wear a leather jacket / ride a motorbike*) while B draws his picture. Students then swap roles and B describes Annabel. Encourage the student who is drawing to ask questions, using *Did he/she use to …?* At the end, students compare their drawings with the originals. Pairs who finish early could go on to make sentences together about the way Alistair and Annabel look now.

◯ Skills focus

(Student's Book page 66)

Exercise 1

• Students look at the photo of Will Murphy. Ask them if they can guess who he is and what he does. How old do they think he is? Ask them to read the text beside the photo to check their answers.

• In pairs, students imagine they are going to interview Will Murphy and prepare a list of questions they want to ask him.

• Ask a few pairs to read out some of their questions.

Exercise 2

• Ask different students to read out the interviewer's questions a–h. Are any of their questions the same?

• Ask students to suggest possible answers for each of these questions.

Exercise 3

• Read through the answers Will Murphy gives to the questions in Exercise 2. Ask students to match them with the answers in Exercise 3. Do the first one with them as an example if necessary.

• Answers are checked in Exercise 4.

Answers	
Answer 1 – question e	Answer 5 – question h
Answer 2 – question d	Answer 6 – question c
Answer 3 – question a	Answer 7 – question f
Answer 4 – question b	Answer 8 – question g

Pronunciation

Exercise 4 ▣ ❸

• a: Play item 3. Students listen and check their answers to Exercise 3.

• b: Ask students to look at the list in Exercise 2 as they listen to the questions again. This time they underline the stressed words in each question. Go through the example with them before they listen to the cassette again.

• c: Point out that stressed words carry the main information. Ask them to check that this is the case with all the words they have underlined.

Answer
See Tapescript.

🔊 TAPESCRIPT

<u>How</u> did you get the <u>part</u> in *Blades*? <u>How</u> did you <u>feel</u> when you <u>got</u> the <u>part</u>? Did you use to be a <u>fan</u> of *Blades* <u>before</u> you got the <u>part</u>? Do you have to be <u>super-fit</u> to <u>play</u> the <u>part</u>? <u>When</u> did you first <u>start</u> rollerblading? Have you been in any <u>other</u> <u>TV shows</u> or <u>films</u>? <u>How</u> do you <u>get on</u> with the <u>other actors</u>? <u>What</u> do you think you'll <u>do</u> <u>next</u>?

Exercise 5

- In each pair, Student A is the interviewer and Student B is Will Murphy.

- Encourage students to use the questions they prepared in Exercise 1, stressing the important words when they ask them. B students should use their imagination to invent Will Murphy's answers. At the end of the interview, they can change roles.

- When they have finished, ask a few pairs to act out their interviews at the front of the class.

⬤ Song

(Student's Book page 67)

Exercise 1

- Students look at the picture and the list of adjectives. What kind of song do they think it is?

Exercise 2

- Start by miming the five moods and ask students to call out the right adjectives. Then switch roles – you say the adjectives (in any order) and students demonstrate the meaning by their expressions and the way they sit.

- Point out the difference between the *-ing* adjective and similar *-ed* adjectives in Exercise 1. Make sure students see that if a song is exciting (= it produces excitement), then you are excited (= you feel the excitement).

- Ask students about the moods in which they feel like singing. Are there particular times and places when they like to sing?

Exercise 3 🔊 ❹

- Read through the questions with the class. Then play the song and let them follow the words as they listen.

- Discuss the questions and ask the students to listen again.

- Replay the song once more and encourage the class to sing along.

🔊 TAPESCRIPT

Walking on Sunshine

I used to think maybe you loved me. Now, baby, I'm sure.
And I just can't wait till the day when you knock on my door
Now every time I go for the mailbox, I gotta hold myself down
Because I just can't wait till you write me you're coming around
I'm walking on sunshine, I'm walking on sunshine
I'm walking on sunshine, and it's time to feel good.
It's time to feel good

I used to think maybe you loved me. Now I know that it's true
But I don't want to spend my whole life just waiting for you
Now, I don't want you back for the weekend, not back for a day
I said baby, I just want you back, and I want you to stay.

I'm walking on sunshine, I'm walking on sunshine
I'm walking on sunshine, and it's time to feel good.
It's time to feel good

⬤ Think about it

(Student's Book page 67)

These sections are a basic round-up of the language taught in the unit. They can be done individually or in pairs in class, or for homework, then checked in the next lesson.

Answers
1 windsurfing e   judo b   swimming a   yoga d
2 *Students' own answers*
3 *Students' own answers*

Workbook answers

❶

2	snow-boarding	6	rock climbing
3	cycling	7	wind surfing
4	weight-training	8	yoga
5	martial arts	9	swimming

❷

1	… had a go?	4	super-fit
2	… get the hang of it.	5	just sitting around
3	I'm really into it.	6	couldn't wait

❸ *Students' own answers*

4

3 They used to drink fizzy drinks.
4 They didn't use to go to aerobics classes.
5 They used to sit around doing nothing.
6 They didn't use to drink water.
7 They didn't use to eat salads.
8 They didn't use to walk to work.
9 They didn't use to cycle to the shops.
10 They used to watch TV for hours.

Buzz words
a aerobics, **b** snow-boarding, **c** cycling,
d weight-training, **e** swimming, **f** rock-climbing,
g windsurfing, **h** martial arts, **i** yoga

5

2 Did she use to go to school? – Yes, she did.
4 Did she use to have an easy life? – No, she didn't.
5 Did she use to write? – No, she didn't.
6 Did she use to be disciplined? – Yes, she did.
7 Did she use to organize her days? – Yes, she did.
8 Did she use to study literature? – No, she didn't.
9 Did she use to walk her dog? – No, she didn't.
10 Did she use to be a champion? – Yes, she did.

6 *Students' own answers*

7

2 What did you use to do in the past / when you were younger?
3 How has your life changed since you've been famous?
4 What other parts have you had on television?
5 How do you get on with other actors?
6 What did you use to think about acting and actors?
7 What's your opinion now?
8 What are your plans for the future?

9

1 He used to have a catering firm in London.
2 He used to spend hours getting to work and back every day.
3 He used to spend time parking, and travelling on trains.
4 He used to stand in crowded places, waiting for the train.
5 He didn't use to shop in local shops.
6 He didn't use to sleep so well.

Coping with exams

Learning objectives

- talking about exam anxieties
- describing feelings
- describing problems and finding solutions
- giving instructions and advice

Language focus

- revision of the present simple
- second conditional
- imperatives

Active vocabulary

anxious	balanced diet	bite
calm	chew	exam
exercise	fit (*adjective*)	nail
organized	panic (*noun*)	plenty of
stress	timetable	upset
vitamin		

Receptive vocabulary

bombardment	bottle up	caffeine
chant	constantly	cry
cut down	disorganized	emotion
exhausted	fizzy drink	increase
jogging	lack (*noun*)	lead-up
mental	mnemonic	multi-coloured
regular	relax	relieve
revise	rhyme	sleepy
social life	technique	tense (*adjective*)
wardrobe	weak	

Materials

Copies of photcopiable page 15 for Additional activity 3.

Pictures or photos of signs and warnings for Additional activity 5.

Lead-ins

a Revise the language from the previous lesson. Get students to tell you something they used to do when they were at primary school.

b Write *examinations* on the board. Students must find as many words as possible using the letters in this word, for example: *man*, *nation*, *next*, etc. See who can come up with the most words.

c Students write a list of exam subjects in English. Put the list on the board, and ask students how they think they will do in these exams.

Vocabulary

(Student's Book page 68)

Exercise 1

- Students look at the pictures, read the questions and discuss them in pairs. Help students with new words or phrases, but do not write these on the board as they will do more on this in Exercise 2.
- Have a brief class feedback session.

Exercise 2

- Refer students to the pictures and give them some practice in using these expressions with *get* and *be*. Make it clear that there is no single meaning for *get*, and let them become familiar with the expressions as set phrases. You might want to point out that in the first and second groups of words, *get* means *become*.
- You could go on to ask students how they react or behave when they get nervous / get tired / can't get enough sleep / don't get any exercise.

Exercise 3

- a: Get students to read the questionnaire quickly. This is a skim-reading exercise, so they only need to match the underlined words and pictures at this stage. They can do this individually or in pairs.

Answers

bite your nails: picture h

chew your pencil: picture d

sometimes cry: picture a

remain calm: picture e

find you can't sleep: picture i

make a timetable: picture g

take regular exercise: picture c

eat a balanced diet: picture b

drink a lot of fizzy drinks: picture f

- b: Ask students to pinpoint the key words that helped them to identify the right pictures. Were there any unfamiliar words that they were able to work out while they were doing the exercise?

Exercise 4

- Now students go through the questionnaire in more detail and answer the questions for themselves. Help them with new words, for example, *lack*, *lips*.
- Get students to discuss their answers with a partner. What do their answers tell them? Are they calm, confident or nervous about exams?
- Have a brief feedback session.

Additional activity 1

Get students to write a list of what they think are the best ways to prepare for an exam. Students compare their answers. Have a class vote on the best advice and write this on the board. Encourage students to use this advice for their exams!

Language focus

(Student's Book page 69)

Exercise 1

- Discuss the meaning of the word *stress*. What are some of the things that cause it and how does it affect people? Why do exams cause stress?
- Students read the title of the article and discuss who they think the article is written for (students preparing for exams).

Exercise 2

- Give students a few minutes to look at the pictures and read the article.
- Students now match the five steps in the article with the pictures. Do the first one with them as an example if necessary.

Answers

1 d 2 c 3 a 4 e 5 b

Exercise 3

- Students now look at the set of five pictures and read the captions. Ask them to decide what each person should do according to the advice in the article. Students can work in pairs or groups.
- Draw attention to the example and point out that students need to use *should* for advice in their answers.

Answers

1 She should get more exercise.
2 He should eat a balanced diet.
3 She should talk to someone.
4 He should make a revision timetable.
5 He should go to bed early.

Focus

- Refer students to the first example and questions a and b. The answer to both questions is no: the second conditional does not refer to present circumstances. Instead, we are talking about a *possibility* that depends on things being different.

- You might also want to point out that this possibility does not feel like a very strong one. Compare the first conditional form (Unit 6): *If she gets more exercise, she'll be able to relax.* Here the possibility seems likely – there is a good chance that it will happen. In the second conditional sentence, the possibility seems more distant and unlikely.

- Draw students' attention to the form of the second conditional. Point out that the two parts of the structure can come in either order – but when the *if* clause comes first, it should be followed by a comma.

Exercise 4

- Students look at the examples referring to the girl in picture 1. Do they agree with the statements?

- Ask them to turn each example round so that the two parts come in the opposite order. Where do they need to put a comma?

Exercise 5

- Either individually or in pairs, students write their own second conditional sentences for the other people in Exercise 3.

- Ask for their answers and write them on the board.

Suggested answers
1 If she got more exercise she would be more relaxed.
2 If he ate a balanced diet, he wouldn't feel weak.
3 If she talked to someone, she wouldn't be suffering from a lot of stress.
4 If he made a revision timetable, he wouldn't be disorganized.
5 If he went to bed early, he wouldn't be sleepy.

Exercise 5

- Ask students to say what they thought about the ideas in the article. Read through the example with them first. In pairs, students discuss their own ideas compared with the ideas in the article.

Additional activity 2

Play 'Noughts and crosses'. Divide the class into two teams and draw up a grid of nine squares on the board. This time, each team must complete a sentence which you read out or write on the board. If they get it wrong, the sentence passes to the other team. If they get it right, they can put a nought or a cross in one of the squares.

Suggested sentences to complete:
If we spoke English really well …
If we lived in America …
If I had a million dollars …
If I found a wallet full of money … (etc.)

Additional activity 3

Pairwork: Make enough copies of photocopiable page 15 for each pair, and cut them into parts A and B. Students take it in turn to ask and answer, referring to the pictures and the prompts provided, and using the second conditional. You could have a feedback session at the end, where students report on their partner's answers (e.g. If she won a lot of money, she would buy a car).

○ Skills focus

(Student's Book page 70)

Exercise 1

- Students describe the pictures in as much detail as they can. Write key words on the board.

- From the pictures, they should deduce that a *swot* is someone who studies really hard, and does little else. A *crammer* is someone who leaves everything to the last minute, then works really hard to 'cram' it in. In pairs, students quickly discuss which one they are more like.

- Have a quick class survey – how many swots and how many crammers are there? Get students to put up their hands.

Exercise 2

- Have a brief class discussion about possible suggestions. They can use their ideas from Additional activity 1 if you did this.

Exercise 3 ▣ ❶

- Read the list of advice with a class. Point out that *cut down on* means 'do less of'. Does the list contain any of their ideas? Can they add anything?

- Students now listen to item 1 and tick the advice they hear.
- Point out that the sentences are all imperatives: they tell you what to do or what not to do. The imperative form is the same as the infinitive.

Answers

Revise as you go along.

Don't leave it to the last minute.

Make a revision timetable.

Cut down on your social life.

Don't stay in every evening.

Keep calm and don't worry.

TAPESCRIPT

Mike And now it's time for 'Exam Tips', our regular ten minute show which gives you advice on how to pass your exams and stay calm. I'm here with Kate Allen, our exam expert. Kate, the exams are still a few months away. What advice have you got for the listeners?

Kate Well, Mike, this week I want to talk about organization and planning. I think it's very important to revise as you go along, you know, throughout the term. Set aside a short revision time after your homework each night.

Mike Good idea!

Kate Whatever you do, don't leave it until the last minute. I think the next important thing is to take a good look at what you need to revise and the dates of your exams. Then make a revision timetable.

Mike I see. What about social life? Should you stop going out in the evenings?

Kate You shouldn't stop going out completely, but as the exams get nearer you should cut down on your social life.

Mike Why shouldn't you stop going out completely?

Kate Well, if you stayed in every evening, you'd get bored and lonely. You wouldn't be able to concentrate on your work.

Mike I see.

Kate Mmm. But most importantly, keep calm and don't worry. Well, I'll be back next week with more advice as the exams get closer.

Mike Yeah, thanks for that, Kate. See you next week. That was Kate Allen with 'Exam Tips' helping you to pass those exams. Next …

▶ **Note**

Caffeine is a drug found in coffee. Ask if they know what else it is found in (tea, cola). Sometimes caffeine is taken out of tea and coffee. This is called *decaffeinated tea/coffee.*

Exercise 4

- In pairs or groups, students discuss what they think of Kate's ideas. Do they think they are practical? What would they themselves suggest?

Additional activity 4

Ask students questions. They must answer with a second conditional. For example:

Why shouldn't you revise with the TV on?
(*If you revised with the TV on, you wouldn't be able to concentrate.*)
Why shouldn't you go to bed late?
(*If you went to bed late, you would feel tired.*)

If you wish, divide the class into two teams and ask the teams alternate questions for a brief class quiz. The team with the most correct answers is the winner.

Additional activity 5

Show students pictures of signs. Students tell you what they mean using imperatives, for example: *Don't smoke. Drive on the right. Don't swim here.*

Exercise 5

- Give students around seven minutes to read the text and to match the techniques a–f with the pictures.
- Discuss some of the vocabulary that may be unfamiliar, encouraging students to try to work out meanings wherever possible. For example, if they recognise the word *bomb* in bombardment, they will be getting close to the basic meaning. *Multi-coloured* is something they might be able to guess from other similar words like *multi-storey* or *multimedia*.
- Ask students to try out the chant in part c, and to make other mnemonics like the one in part a for short lists of words.

Answers

1 e 2 b 3 c 4 a 5 d 6 f

Exercise 6

- In pairs, students discuss the best techniques from Exercise 5 to learn these topics for an English exam. There are no right or wrong answers, but students should give reasons for their choices.

- Encourage students to use some or all of these techniques for their revision.

Additional activity 5

Dictate the following sentence to the class:

The quick brown fox jumps over the lazy dog.

How many letters of the alphabet can they find in this sentence? (It includes all of them.) Get them to say each letter as they find it.

Exercise 7

- Students discuss the question in pairs, then have a class discussion about their answers.

- Give a suggestion yourself if you can. For example, to remember the word *teapot*, can they think of a word in their language which sounds similar?

Exercise 8

- Students write their own magazine feature called 'Revision Techniques'.

- Encourage them to use the information from this unit but also to include their own examples and techniques.

- Features can be displayed on the walls.

○ **Think about it!**

(Student's Book page 71)

These sections are a basic round-up of the language taught in the unit. They can be done individually or in pairs in class, or for homework, then checked in the next lesson.

Suggested answers

1 They bite their lips. They chew their pencil. They play with their hair.

2 They should eat a balanced diet. They should avoid staying up very late at night. They should talk to people.

3 b She'd be better organized if she made a revision timetable.

   c If she didn't drink coffee, she'd be able to sleep.

Workbook answers

Buzz words

Positive	Negative
confident	nervous
calm	anxious
organized	sleepy
fit	upset

❶ *Students' own answers*

❷

drink: I should drink lots of water. I shouldn't drink too much tea or coffee.
rest: I should get lots of rest.
exercise: I should try to do lots of exercise.
revision: I should make a realistic revision timetable and stick to it. I shouldn't revise for too long without a break.

Students' own answers

❸

2 He would have friends if he didn't treat people so badly.

3 He would have some money if he didn't spend it all on computer games.

4 He would get invited to parties if he didn't make trouble.

5 He would pass his tests if he didn't miss classes and studied more.

7 His classmates wouldn't like him if he wasn't/weren't so friendly with everyone, and didn't share things.

8 He wouldn't be invited to all the parties if he wasn't/weren't such great fun.

9 He wouldn't do so well at school if he didn't work so hard.

10 He wouldn't be such a good runner if he didn't train so hard.

❹

1 if you took notes

2 spend all your money on sweets and stickers, you'd have enough money to buy the book

3 you would lend me the money

4 feel sick if you stopped eating five bars of chocolate every morning

5 don't get the sugar; feel

6 would have time to eat breakfast

7 you got up earlier

❺

2 If I didn't have to go to school, I would …

3 If I had £500 to spend any way I liked, I would …

4 If my best friend moved to another town, I would …

5 If I could stay up at night, I would …

❻

Organization, Food, Rest, Drinks, Keeping active, Feelings

❼

1 I would buy a computer; I would go to America; I would go on holiday with my friends.

2 I would drive to pick up my girlfriend in the evening; I would drive to different towns; I wouldn't have to wait for the bus anymore.

3 They would buy me a guitar; They wouldn't be upset with me; I would be able to have a party to celebrate.

Revision

Units 11–15

Stop and think!

The exercises and activities in this unit revise all the language taught in Units 11–15. It is divided into five sections. The HELP screen suggests extra help or activities. Encourage students to refer to these while they are working or set them as homework. When they can do each section, students can colour the letters.

Describing feelings

(Student's Book page 72)

- Ask students to complete the sentences with a suitable adjective from the list. Encourage them to use a dictionary or give help with vocabulary if necessary.

Answers

1 afraid   2 moody   3 optimistic   4 pessimistic
5 embarrassed   6 Confident   7 jealous   8 shy

Present perfect/simple past

(Student's Book page 73)

Exercise 1

- Look at the first picture. Practise the short dialogue with whole class and review past simple / present perfect forms: *I've seen it. I went with Sue last week.* In pairs, students look at pictures 1–5 and decide on the correct form of the verbs.

- Elicit the correct answers and write them on the board. Allow students time to copy the correct answers into their books.

Answers

1 I haven't done / didn't do; had to
2 The dog's eaten / The dog ate; heard
3 I've been; made
4 They've gone / They went; told.
5 I haven't fed; forgot

Exercise 2

- Students write sentences about their own experiences, following the example.

Present perfect questions

(Student's Book page 73)

Exercise 1

- Ask students to complete the table individually and compare their answers in pairs.

- Go through the table with the whole class, eliciting the answers and writing them on the board.

Answers

drank/drunk, ate/eaten, forgot/forgotten, had/had, made/made, met/met, rode/ridden, saw/seen, slept/slept

Exercise 2

- Remind students of the concept of *Have you ever ...?* meaning 'at any time of your life until now'. Ask them to check through vocabulary themselves and explain anything unfamiliar to them. Drill the example question and answer, paying attention to stress and intonation.

- Get students to write the questions for 1–8, working alone or in pairs as you wish. Go around and monitor for accuracy.

- In pairs, students take it in turn to ask their questions. They should reply with true answers, *Yes I have / No I haven't.*

Answers

Have you ever ...

1 eaten snake? (Point out that *snake* here is uncountable and means the meat.)
2 ... met a famous person?
3 ... had a nightmare?
4 ... ridden a horse?
5 ... failed an exam?
6 ... drunk too much coffee?
7 ... forgotten your name?
8 ... slept in a tent?

- To extend this, you can ask students to write three more *Have you ever ...?* questions. When they have finished, get them to go around the class putting their questions to as many people as possible. If they get a positive answer, they should ask the other student for more information using the past simple. For example:

A Have you ever lost a lot of money?
B Yes I have.
A How much did you lose? (etc.)

used to

(Student's Book page 74)

- Ask students to look at the information about Mrs Godfrey. Focus on the example sentence below and model the pronunciation. Revise the concept of *used to* by asking: *Is she rich now? Was she rich in the past?*

- Ask students to use the rest of the prompts to make more sentences about Mrs Godfrey's life. They should write them in their notebooks and check answers with a partner.

- Go over the answers with the whole class.

Answers

She used to live in a very big house but now she lives in a tiny flat.

She used to drive a Rolls Royce but now she hasn't got a car.

She used to eat in restaurants every day but now she never eats in restaurants.

She used to go on holiday three times a year but now can't afford to go on holiday.

She used to be invited to lots of big parties but now she is never invited to parties.

She used to know lots of famous people but now her old friends don't talk to her.

Exercise 2

- Students work individually to write the sentences, and then check in pairs. Go over the answers with the whole class.

Answers

1 They used to live in Manchester.
2 I used to love it.
3 It used to be exciting.
4 We used to go every week.

Second conditional

(Student's Book page 74)

Exercise 1

- Revise the form and function of the second conditional, for example: *If I won a lot of money, I would travel around the world* (it is possible but it probably won't happen).

- Get students to work in pairs and complete the exercise, joining the two halves of the sentences with *would* or *wouldn't*.

- Go over the answers with the whole class. Use the completed sentences for more oral practice, paying special attention to stress and intonation.

Exercise 2

- Focus students' attention on the first picture and example sentence. Get them to look at pictures 1–4 and rewrite the matching sentences using the second conditional. Students compare answers with a partner.

Answers

1 If I liked horror movies, I'd go with you.
2 If the boots weren't too small, he'd buy them.
3 If the car were bigger, they'd all fit in.
4 If she weren't so/very busy, she'd answer the door.

Exercise 3

- Encourage students to use their imagination and complete the sentences. Put them into groups of four to compare their ideas.

Reading and writing

(Student's Book page 75)

Exercises 1 and 2

- Write the first three questions in Exercise 2 on the board and ask students what they think the story might be about. Then either let them read the story or read it aloud to them. Get students to talk in pairs about their answers to the questions.

- Students should read the text again and write down their answers. They can discuss question 4 in pairs or small groups for two or three minutes.

- Elicit suggestions and discuss with the whole class.

Exercise 3

- Students talk about their dreams in small groups. Ask them to make notes about a particular dream they remember. They can write about it in class or as homework.

Project idea

(Student's Book page 75)

- Introduce the idea of keeping a 'Dream Diary' using the suggestions on page 75. Encourage students to do this and see if they can describe their dreams in English. They may like to read each other's diaries and try to say what they think the dreams mean.

- Remind students to keep the diary over the coming weeks and allow time for discussion in a month's time.

Projects

Films

Active vocabulary

comedy	Doomed	Forbidden
love story	special effects	stars

Receptive vocabulary

aboard	allowed	dramatic
ending	excellent	forgetful
handsome	girlfriend	plot
poor	sad	scientist
sinking	stuff	wedding
realistic		

Materials

Large sheets of paper, coloured pens and pencils.

Lead-in

Write the categories, *comedy*, *love story*, *action film*, *science fiction* on the board. Elicit examples of each type of film and write them on the board. Give the students five minutes to think of as many film titles for each category as they can in groups. The group with the most correct film titles is the winner.

Exercise 1

- Look at the photos on the page with the class.
- In pairs, students try to name the photos on the page.
- Listen to their ideas with the class.

Answers

Star Wars, Spice World, Batman and Robin, Jurassic Park, Anastasia, Indiana Jones, Tomorrow Never Dies.

Exercise 2

- Invite a few students to tell you about their favourite films
- In pairs, students tell each other about their favourite films.

Exercise 3

- Look at the film posters on the page with the class.
- Ask the students if they have seen either of these films and which they would like to go and see.

Exercise 4

- Go through any difficult vocabulary with the class.
- Students read the texts and match the correct caption with the correct text.

Answers

Forbidden love on doomed ship – *Titanic*
A comedy for all the family – *Flubber*

Exercise 5

- Look at the table with the class.
- Show the students where the information in the table came from.
- Draw the table on the board.
- In pairs, students work together to find the missing information. The first pair to find all the answers is the winner.
- Students report back the answers. Listen and fill in the table on the board.

Exercise 6

- Tell students about a film you like and fill in the table on the board with information about it.
- Students work in pairs to fill in the table with information about a film they have seen at the cinema, on TV, or know about.

Exercise 7

- Look back at the film review posters with the class. Point out the paragraph describing the film, the caption and the picture.
- Working in groups, students use the information in their table to make illustrated film review posters like the ones for *Flubber* and *Titanic*.

Exercise 8

- Display the film posters on the classroom wall.
- Have a class vote to see which is the best one.

Projects

Game shows

Active vocabulary

game shows   hexagon   prize
watching

Receptive vocabulary

competitor   fight   Gladiators
hurt   Individual players   race
series   show   sports car
strong

Materials

Small pieces of card and objects which the students could use as counters.

Lead-in

Have a class grammar game show. Divide the class into two teams. Write ten grammatically incorrect sentences on the board. Ask both teams to point out the mistakes in five different sentences, in turn. Award each team a point for every mistake they spot. If they get the answer wrong, give the other team an opportunity to answer. The team with the most points is the winner.

Exercise 1

- Look at the photos of game shows with the class.
- Ask the students if they recognize any of them.
- In pairs, student discuss the questions.
- Invite students to tell you the results of their discussions.

Exercise 2

- In pairs, give students a short amount of time to make a list of all the TV game shows they can think of.
- The pair with the most game shows on their list is the winner.

Exercise 3

- Look at the photos with the class. Ask if anyone knows the name of the game show.
- Invite students to suggest what is happening in the photos.
- Ask the students if they would like to go on this game show.

Exercise 4

- Students read the text and answer the question.
- Go round the class helping with any difficult vocabulary.
- Check the answer with the class.

Answers

The prize is usually a sports car or a motorcycle.

Exercise 5

- Divide each group into two teams.
- Look at the board game and question cards with the class. Point out to the students that the answer to each question begins with a letter on the board.
- Each team writes a question for every letter on the game board on separate pieces of card.

Exercise 6

- Students play the game. The aim of the game is for each team to reach the other side of the board first. Each team must try to block the other team's path to the other side by moving onto hexagons in the other team's path. Only one team is allowed on each hexagon at a time.
- Team A starts at one end of the board on a hexagon.
- Team B asks Team A question about that letter. If Team A gets the question right, they move onto an adjoining hexagon of their choice and Team B asks them another question.
- When Team A gets a question wrong, Team B moves onto a hexagon and answers a question about that letter.

Projects

Food

Active vocabulary

cafe	dessert	main course
menu	preference	

Receptive vocabulary

apple pie	carrot	chips
chocolate cake	fruit salad	new potatoes
pizza	raspberry sauce	salmon
soup of the day	spaghetti	steak
tomato soup		

Materials

Paper and coloured pens and pencils.

Lead-in

Have a food brainstorming session. Brainstorm different types of food and write them on the board.

Exercise 1

- Look at the photos with the class.
- Check that the students know all the vocabulary. Refer to the brainstormed words on the board and draw pictures if necessary.
- Invite students to tell you which of the foods they like and don't like.
- Students work in pairs, discussing foods they like and don't like.

Exercise 2

- Look at the survey with the class.
- Check that the students know all the vocabulary.
- Invite students to tell you which foods they want to use to complete their survey.
- Students work in pairs to ask and answer about their food preferences.

Exercise 3

- Have a class feedback session. Draw the survey table on the board and add all the possible different categories. Write the results of the surveys on the board and find out which is the most popular food in your class.

Exercise 4

- Look at the two menus with the class. Check that the students know what *Starter*, *Main Course* and *Dessert* mean.
- In pairs, students discuss which of the menus they like best.
- Students should use their dictionaries but go round the class helping where necessary.
- Invite students to tell you which menu they like best and why.

Exercise 5

- Students work in pairs to discuss and create a menu for an imaginary cafe or restaurant. Encourage students to decorate their menus with illustrations.

Exercise 6

- Display the menus on the classroom wall.
- Have a class vote to see which is the most popular menu.

Projects

Magazines

Active vocabulary

letters page

magazine

pop star questionnaire

puzzle and jokes page

Receptive vocabulary

lies

problems

stupid

world tour

Materials

Paper, pens and coloured pencils.

Lead-in

Write the words *Teenage Magazines* on the board. In pairs, students try to make as many words as possible out of the two words. The pair with the most correct words is the winner.

Exercise 1

- Look at the photos with the class. Ask the class what sort of age of people they think these magazines are for.
- In pairs, students discuss the types of things you would find in a magazine for teenagers; questionnaires, interviews, song lyrics, articles, problem pages, letter pages, quizzes, photos, horoscopes etc.
- Listen to their suggestions and write them on the board.

Exercise 2

- Ask the students if they read magazines like this. In pairs, students discuss what they like about them.
- Invite a few students to tell you what they like about teenage magazines and write it on the board.

Exercise 3

- Students read the star interview and answer the question.

Answers

nothing/a holiday

Exercise 4

- Students read the HOT! letters page.
- Go round the class, helping with vocabulary.
- In pairs, students choose a letter and write a short reply.
- Invite students to read out their replies.

Exercise 5

- In groups, students write and produce a magazine.
- Remind students of all the things you would find in a magazine for teenagers.
- Organize the groups into pairs and let the students decide what each pair in their group should do.
- Whilst they are working, pairs from different groups can get together to share ideas.
- Students think of a name for their magazine and design a cover.

Exercise 6

- Each group should present their magazine to the class.
- Students walk round the class, reading each others magazines.
- Have a class vote on which is the best one. Have different categories, such as best design and best articles, as well as an overall winner.

Photocopiable pages

The next 30 pages of this Teacher's Book may be photocopied for use in the classroom.

Photocopiable pages 1 – 15

Pairwork activities

Photocopiable pages 16 – 30

A full-page photocopiable test for each unit

Photocopiable page 1

Student A

Read the questions and answers. Match the answers to some of the questions and try to answer the other questions. Then read the questions with Student B. Ask each other for the answers you do not have. See how many you get right! Good luck!

Quiz time!

1 What is the highest mountain in the world? ....

2 How high is the highest mountain in the world? ....

3 Where do giant tortoises live? ....

4 Where is the Sea of Tranquillity? ....

5 Which river goes through London, the capital of England? ....

6 Which star is closest to Earth? ....

7 Which river goes through Cairo, the capital of Egypt? ....

8 What is the name of the smallest country in the world? ....

9 How far does a police officer usually walk in a year? ....

10 How fast can a blue shark swim? ....

11 How many babies does a mother dolphin have at one time? ....

12 How many legs has an insect got? ....

Answers
a Six.
b 8,848 metres.
c The Nile.
d On the moon.
e About 69 km per hour.
f The sun.

✂- -

Student B

Read the quiz questions and answers. Match the answers to some of the questions and try to answer the other questions. Then read the questions with Student A. Ask each other for the answers you do not have. See how many you get right! Good luck!

Quiz time!

1 What is the highest mountain in the world? ....

2 How high is the highest mountain in the world? ....

3 Where do giant tortoises live? ....

4 Where is the Sea of Tranquillity? ....

5 Which river goes through London, the capital of England? ....

6 Which star is closest to Earth? ....

7 Which river goes through Cairo, the capital of Egypt? ....

8 What is the name of the smallest country in the world? ....

9 How far does a police officer usually walk in a year? ....

10 How fast can a blue shark swim? ....

11 How many babies does a mother dolphin have at one time? ....

12 How many legs has an insect got? ....

Answers
a One.
b The Thames.
c Mount Everest.
d About 2,626 km.
e Vatican City (where the Pope lives).
f The Galapagos Islands (in South America).

Photocopiable page 2

With your partner, read each sentence and decide if it is true or false. Put a tick in the correct box. Then answer the question. For example:

	True	False
A lot of British people drink coffee with milk or cream.	✓	☐

What do people drink with coffee in your country? ...*Sugar, but no milk.*........

	True	False
1 British people usually say 'Good appetite!' at the beginning of a meal.	☐	☐
What do you say?		
2 Most British people eat meat, eggs and bread for breakfast.	☐	☐
What do most people eat for breakfast in your country?		
3 A lot of people in Britain drink tea.	☐	☐
What do you like drinking?		
4 A lot of British people do not put sugar in their tea.	☐	☐
What do people in your country put in their tea?		
5 The British take two or three hours for lunch.	☐	☐
How long do you take for lunch?		
6 The most important meal of the day in Britain is dinner.	☐	☐
What is the most important meal of the day in your country?		
7 The British eat most of their food with their fingers.	☐	☐
What food do you eat with your fingers?		
8 The British usually eat dinner at about seven or eight o'clock in the evening.	☐	☐
What time do you have dinner?		
9 If British people eat at a friend's house, they say 'Mmm. This is delicious.' to show that they like the food.	☐	☐
Do you say anything? What do you say?		
10 In Britain, it is polite to eat with your mouth open and speak with food in your mouth.	☐	☐
What about in your country?		
11 The British sometimes eat ice cream at the end of a meal.	☐	☐
What do people in your country eat at the end of a meal?		
12 In Britain bread is served with every meal.	☐	☐
Is something served with every meal in your country? What?		

Photocopiable page 3

Student A

You and Student B have some pictures showing different parts of an action movie. The man's name is Matt and the woman's name is Rose.

Take it in turns to describe your pictures. Make notes in your blank squares.

Then work with Student B and put all the pictures into the correct order. Number them 1–12

Student B

You and Student A have some pictures showing different parts of an action movie. The man's name is Matt and the woman's name is Rose.

Take it in turns to describe your pictures. Make notes in your blank squares.

Then work with Student A and put all the pictures into the correct order. Number them 1–12

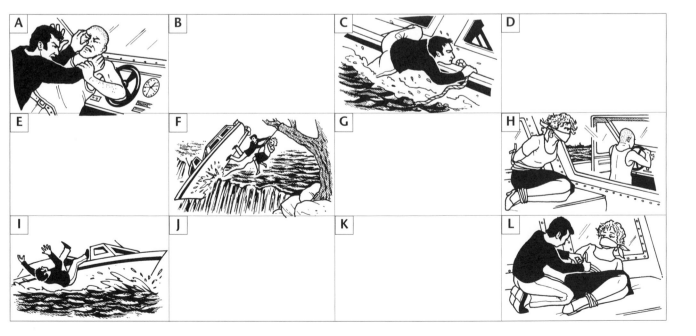

Jim lived in a small house outside London with his parents. Every day, his father got up early and drove himself to work in his shiny, new car.

f   This was wonderful news! Mike and Jim went to pick up the car. They found a strange note on the front seat.

a   They saw a very funny musical and really enjoyed themselves. However, when they arrived home, they got the biggest shock of their lives! The family's TV, video player, computer and CD player were all gone!

g   However, Mike was very surprised and angry that morning! Why?

h   It said, 'Sorry I took your car. It was very important for me to get home quickly last night. I hope you weren't too angry. Please accept these theatre tickets as a thank you from me.'

b   Mike ran up and down the street, looking for his beautiful car. After half an hour, he went back inside the house and telephoned the police.

i   Who did this? Well, there was a note which said, 'Now you know why I gave you the theatre tickets. The Gentleman Thief.'

c   One day, Jim's father, Mike, got up, had breakfast, said goodbye and left the house to drive to work. As usual.

j   When Jim got home that afternoon, the phone rang. It was the police. The car was outside the police station!

d   Because his car was not parked outside on the street. He was sure it was there yesterday, but that morning it was gone!

k   After phoning, Mike caught the train to work and Jim got to school late. He didn't want to study because he felt too sad. His father loved that car!

e   Who wrote the note? The police didn't know and Jim's dad didn't know, either! What a gentleman the thief was, they thought. So they decided to go to the theatre that Saturday evening.

© Oxford University Press 1998

Photocopiable page 5

Student A

Complete the story. Ask Student B to dictate the missing words in the first sentence to you. Ask for help with the spelling if necessary. Then dictate the words you have in this sentence to Student B. Continue with the other sentences.

When you finish, check your answers together. Then read the story again – and enjoy!

VILLAIN OR HERO?

Micky Curtis was .... and famous

film star. .... very attractive and he

.... beautifully.

.... one big problem, however. He

.... friends easily. He told ....

.... what to do and ....

.... at the other actors.

Micky talked happily about only .... :

himself. He talked about his money, ...

.... , fast cars and ....

....

One afternoon, he was filming .... the film

In Search of the Blue Diamond. A young camerawoman

.... to move. Micky

looked at her angrily and ....

....

'Do you know who .... ?

I'm the best actor and .... in

the world. I've got ....

What have you got?'

The camerawoman looked at Micky. Then she

.... happily, '.......... .... friends!'

Student B

Complete the story. First dictate the words you have in the first sentence to Student A. Then ask Student A to dictate the missing words in this sentence to you . Ask for help with the spelling if necessary. Continue with the other sentences.

When you finish, check your answers together. Then read the story again – and enjoy!

VILLAIN OR HERO?

Micky Curtis was a very rich and ....

.... He was ....

.... and he acted ....

There was one .... , however. He did

not make .... He told film

directors .... and he shouted angrily .....

....

Micky .... about only one

thing: himself. He talked about .... , his

big houses, ... and private planes.

.... , he was filming part of

the film *In Search of the Blue Diamond*. A young

camerawoman asked him politely ....

Micky ....

and started shouting loudly.

'..... .... you are talking to? I'm

.... and the richest man in the

world. I've got millions of dollars. What ....

.... ?'

The camerawoman looked at Micky. Then she

answered .... , 'I've got .... !'

Student A

Ask your partner questions and complete the table.
Find a suitable penfriend for each person.

Penfriend's Club

name	Becky	Joanne	Ahmet	Paul	Sam	Maria
age	12		11			10
lives		England		Scotland	America	
sports/ hobbies	watching TV		cycling football running			sailing swimming
ideal penfriend needs to		like all water sports		like football and playing outdoors	like having fun	

✂ ---

Student B

Ask your partner questions and complete the table.
Find a suitable penfriend for each person.

Penfriend's Club

name	Becky	Joanne	Ahmet	Paul	Sam	Maria
age		10		11	11	
lives	England		Turkey			Greece
sports/ hobbies		swimming surfing		football	watching TV	
ideal penfriend needs to	be good fun		like playing games outside			like going to the beach

© Oxford University Press 1998

Photocopiable page 7

Student A

You are a teacher. Student B is going to ask you questions about your daily routine to find out your job. Use the chart to answer his/her questions.

Questions	Student A	Student B
time/start/work?	8.30	
How/travel/work?	bus or walk	
wear uniform/smart clothes?	smart clothes	
time/finish/work?	4.30	
work/other people?	children	
enjoy?	sometimes	

Use the chart to help you interview Student B about his/her daily routine. Can you guess what Student B's job is?

Student B

Use the chart to help you interview Student A about his/her daily routine. Can you guess what Student A's job is?

Questions	Student A	Student B
time/start/work?		sometimes morning/sometimes evening
How/travel/work?		bus
wear uniform/smart clothes?		always/uniform
time/finish work		sometimes morning/sometimes evening
work/other people?		adults and children
enjoy?		usually

You are a nurse. Student A is going to ask you questions about your daily routine to find out your job. Use the chart to answer his/her questions.

Photocopiable page 8

Student A

Read about William's letter. Work with Student B to put the sentences in the right order. Write their number in the box.

a   The letter is posted in the post box. ☐

b   The letters are posted through the letter box. ☐

c   The letters are put on a train. ☐

d   The post box is emptied by the postman. ☐

e   The letters are taken to the sorting ofice. ☐

f   The stamp is bought from the post office. ☐

g   They are taken to the post office. ☐

h   They are delivered to the door by the postman. ☐

i   The letter is written by William. ☐1

j   William's letter is opened by Anna. ☐

✂ -

Student B

Describe the pictures to help Student A put the sentences in the right order. Write the letter in the box.

1 ☐   2 ☐   3 ☐   4 ☐   5 ☐

6 ☐   7 ☐   8 ☐   9 ☐   10 ☐

© Oxford University Press 1998

Photocopiable page 9

Student A

Someone robbed the bank in Northridge at the time of the earthquake. Ask Student B what the following people were doing and find out the name of the thief.

Gary Sledge

Mike Lane

Jim Nightingale

Steve Smith

What was Gary Sledge doing at the time of the earthquake?

Jennifer MacRobie

Robert MacRobie

Kate Gray

✂ -

Student B

Someone robbed the bank in Northridge at the time of the earthquake. Ask Student A what the following people were doing and find out the name of the thief.

Robert MacRobie

Jennifer MacRobie

Steve Smith

Kate Gray

What was Robert MacRobie doing at the time of the earthquake?

Gary Sledge

Mike Lane

Jim Nightingale

Photocopiable page 10

Student A

Complete the crossword by asking student B questions.

▶ A What is 2 across?
   B This is something that comes from trees. What is 1 down?
▶ A T-shirts are made of this.

Use these clues to help Student B complete his/her crossword. Don't tell them the answers!

Across

4 Drinks cans are made of this.
6 This means the opposite of artificial.
8 These are things we throw away.
11 Our planet.

Down

1 T-shirts are made of this.
9 Elephants are killed to get this.

Student B

Complete the crossword by asking Student A questions.

   A What is 2 across?
▶ B This is something that comes from trees. What is 1 down?
   A T-shirts are made of this.

Use these clues to help Student A complete his/her crossword. Don't tell them the answers!

Across

2 Something that comes from trees.
3 Something that is made from oil.
7 Something that is made of glass or plastic.
12 Tyres are made of this.

Down

5 Shoes are made of this.
10 Something that is made from wood.

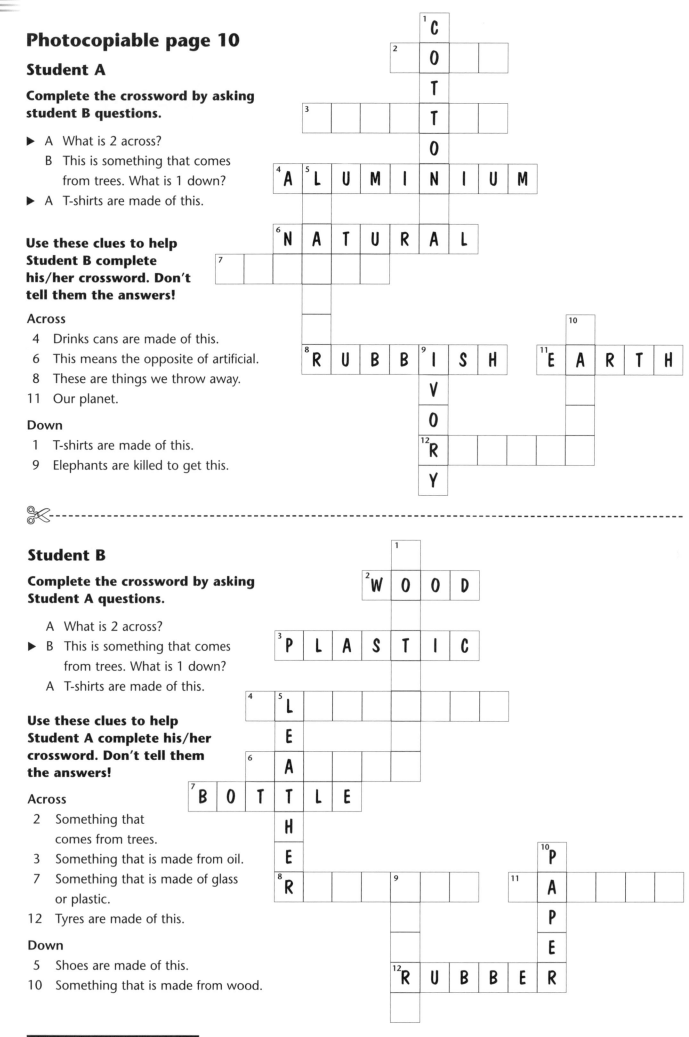

Photocopiable page 11

Student A

Work with Student B and find the two sentences that belong in Student B's letter.

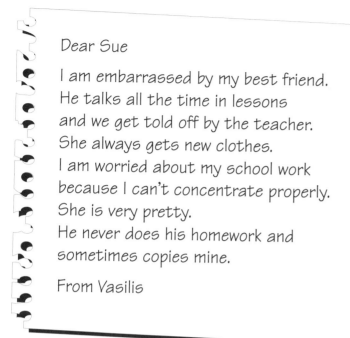

Dear Sue

I am embarrassed by my best friend.
He talks all the time in lessons
and we get told off by the teacher.
She always gets new clothes.
I am worried about my school work
because I can't concentrate properly.
She is very pretty.
He never does his homework and
sometimes copies mine.

From Vasilis

Student B

Work with Student B and find the two sentences that belong in Student A's letter.

Dear Sue

I am jealous of my best friend.
My mum wants me to move desks.
She is confident and I am very shy.
It's making me sad and moody.
She wants me to sit with
someone who is quiet and works hard.
She asks me what is wrong but I
don't want to tell her.

From Christina

Photocopiable page 12

Student A

Your friend Jason has told you lots of things that he has done. Make questions and find out from Student B if they are true. For example:

Has he been to America?

Write ✓ (yes) or ✗ (no) in each box.

1 be/America?

2 fly/aeroplane?

3 drive/car?

4 meet/film star?

Use the pictures to answer Student B's questions about Kylie.

No, she hasn't been to America, but she's been to France.

Student B

Your friend Kylie has told you lots of things that she has done. Make questions and find out from Student A if they are true. For example:

Has she flown in a hot-air balloon?

Write ✓ (yes) or ✗ (no) in each box.

1 fly/hot-air balloon?

2 be/pop concert?

3 travel/train?

4 be/America?

Use the pictures to answer Student A's questions about Jason.

No, he hasn't flown a plane, but he's sailed a boat.

Photocopiable page 13

Student A

**Look at the sentences about a dream. Listen to
Student B and put the sentences in the correct
order.**

a   A man is walking down a long, dark tunnel.   ☐1

b   He is flying like a bird.   ☐

c   He is getting into a small boat.   ☐

d   He is swimming under water.   ☐

e   He is walking on the beach.   ☐

f   He is sleeping in a field of flowers.   ☐

g   He is diving into the sea.   ☐

h   He is climbing up a mountain.   ☐

Student B

**The pictures show a dream sequence. Describe
the dream and help Student A put the
sentences in the right order.**

Photocopiable page 14

Student A

Look at the picture of Alistair. Tell Student B what he used to look like. For example:

He used to have long hair.

Listen to Student B describe what Annabel used to look like and draw her picture. When you have both finished, compare your drawings.

Student B

Listen to Student A describe what Alistair used to look like and draw his picture.

Look at the picture of Annabel. Tell Student A what she used to look like. For example:

She used to wear big earrings.

When you have both finished, compare your drawings.

Photocopiable page 15

Student A

Look at the top three pictures and ask Student B questions. For example:

What would you do if you won a lot of money?

1 won/money
2 met/famous person
3 fell/love

Use the other pictures to answer Student B's questions.

a go/hospital
b sunbathe/pool
c stay/bed

Student B

Use the top three pictures to answer Student A's questions.

a buy/car
b ask/autograph
c get/married

Look at the other pictures and ask Student A questions. For example:

What would you do if you injured your leg?

1 injured/ leg
2 won/holiday
3 had/day off school

Photocopiable page 16

UNIT 1 TEST

1 Listen to your teacher and draw the weird animal. It has parts of the body from many different animals.

MARK: ....../6

2 Complete the questions.

1 <u>How tall</u>.............. is a lion? A metre?

2 .... does a blue whale weigh?

3 .... legs does a bee have? Six or eight?

4 .... can polar bears run?

5 .... bird is the fastest?

6 .... can a tortoise walk in an hour?

7 .... does a baby whale stay with its mother? For a month?

8 .... babies does a snake have? Four?

9 .... do crocodiles sleep? In the water?

MARK: ....../8

3 Write the questions for these answers. Use the verbs in the list. One verb is used twice

travel	have	got	come	run	be	hear

1 .....<u>Can</u>...... polar bears ...<u>run</u>..... fast?
Yes, they can.

2 .... whales .... in groups?
Yes, they do.

3 .... any vampire bats in Europe?
No, there aren't.

4 .... crocodiles .... well under water?
No, they can't.

5 .... spiders .... eyes?
Yes, they have.

6 .... this kind of spider dangerous?
Yes, it is.

7 .... the tortoise .... from Australia?
No, it doesn't.

MARK: ....../6

TOTAL: ....../20

Photocopiable page 17

UNIT 2 TEST

1 Listen to your teacher and complete the recipe.

1 .....Cut......... some rolls in half.

2 .... butter on them.

3 .... an apple into small pieces and .... the pieces with some cheese.

4 .... the mixture on the rolls.

5 .... some mayonnaise.

6 .... the sandwiches cold until you are ready to eat them.

MARK: ....../6

2 Put the words in the correct columns.

> corn   chicken   rice   chillies   yoghurt
> potatoes   beef   oil   cheese

Grain   Fruit and vegetables

.corn..........................   ....

....

....

Dairy products   Meat and fish

....

....

....

Other

....

MARK: ....../8

3 Complete the sentences with *is/are* + *filled/made/served*.

1 My favourite cake ...is made.............. with flour, eggs, butter, sugar and chocolate.

2 In India yoghurt .... with curry.

3 These sandwiches .... with tuna and mayonnaise.

4 This curry .... with vegetables, spices and garlic.

5 .... this omelette .... with mushrooms?

6 I like these hamburgers because they .... with lots of meat.

7 All our dishes .... with salad.

MARK: ....../6

TOTAL: ....../20

UNIT 3 TEST

1 Look at the pictures and complete the sentences.

1 .....She's going to..... .....jump out of.....

the plane.

2 ....

his horse.

3 ....

the river.

4 ....

the cliff.

5 ....

the bridge.

6 ....

the wall.

MARK: ....../10

2 Write questions for the answers.

1 ...Are you going ti have stunts in the film?......

Yes, we're going to have five stunts.

2 ....

Yes, they're going to be very dangerous!

3 ....

No, Kevin isn't going to do all the stunts.

4 ....

He's going to practise his stunt tomorrow morning at eight.

5 ....

He's going to ride at about 100 kilometres per hour.

6 ....

No, they aren't. They're going to film the stunt on Tuesday, not tomorrow.

MARK: ....../10

TOTAL: ....../20

© Oxford University Press 1998

Photocopiable page 19

UNIT 4 TEST

1 Complete the sentences with the verbs in brackets. Use the verbs in the past or the present.

My parents sometimes [1] ..**take**.......... (take) me and my sisters to the theatre. Last week they [2] .... (take) us to a play by Shakespeare. It was Saturday night and we [3] .... (go) to an open-air theatre in the park. Every summer actors [4] .... (perform) Shakespeare plays there. They [5] .... (use) the trees as part of the scenery.

On Saturday we [6] .... (see) the play called *A Midsummer Night's Dream*. There [7] .... (not be) any famous actors in it, but it [8] .... (be) very good. Some of the actresses [9] .... (wear) beautiful costumes.

It [10] .... (not rain), but it [11] .... (begin) to get cold in the last part of the play.

MARK: ....../10

2 Complete the labels.

1 _ i _ g _ _

2 _ c _ n _ _ y

3 s _ _ _ e

4 _ _ _ t s

5 a _ d _ _ _ _ e

MARK: ...../5

3 Write the past forms of these verbs.

1 see   ..**saw**..............

2 catch   ....

3 buy   ....

4 fall   ....

5 tell   ....

6 make   ....

MARK: ...... /5

TOTAL: ...... /20

Photocopiable page 20

UNIT 5 TEST

1 Write the opposite of these adjectives.

1 young   .old..................

2 tall   ....

3 attractive   ....

4 intelligent   ....

5 friendly   ....

6 fat   ....

MARK: ....../5

2 Complete the sentences with *is/are* or *look/looks* and the adjectives in the list.

| intelligent   calm   fat   worried   tall |
| friendly   attractive |

1 She ......looks......
......friendly........ .

2 They ....
....

3 He ....
....

4 They ....
....

5 He ....
....

6 She ....
....

7 She ....
....

Mark: ...../6

3 Complete the sentences with the adverbs in the list.

| carefully   worriedly   slowly   clearly |
| politely   nervously |

1 'Are you all right? Are you safe? Have you got enough food?' he asked ...worriedly........... .

2 She doesn't usually sing .... so I can't hear the words in her songs.

3 They answered his questions .... because they were scared of him.

4 I'm eating .... because I don't like the food much.

5 'Thank you very much for a delicious meal,' he said ....

6 Next time I will check my homework very .... to find the mistakes.

MARK: ....../5

4 Match these verbs from Exercise 3 with the tenses.

1 he asked   past simple
                         – irregular verb

2 she doesn't sing   *will*

3 he said   present continuous

4 I'm eating   past simple
                         – regular verb

5 I will check   present simple

MARK: ...../4

TOTAL: ....../20

Photocopiable page 21

UNIT 6 TEST

1 Name the hobbies. Label the pictures with the words below.

1 ....
2 ....
3 ....
4 ....
5 ....
6 ....
7 ....
8 ....

aerobics football making jewellery making models horse-riding chess playing an instrument stamp collecting

MARK: ..../8

2 Look at the information in this prospectus about the pottery club. Make sentences using *need to/have to* or *needn't /don't have to*.

> Our school is proud of its pottery club. You can make beautiful pots on our wheels, or your very own sculptures. You don't need to know about pottery but you need enthusiasm. You have to bring an apron because pottery can be messy, but you needn't bring your own tools. You don't have to be artistic but it helps! You have to pay a fee of £10 but you needn't pay it until 15th September.

1 You ...*don't have to*.......... know about pottery.

2 You .... enthusiasm.

3 You .... bring an apron.

4 You .... bring your own tools.

5 You .... artistic.

6 You .... to pay a fee.

7 You .... pay it by 15th September.

MARK: ..../6

3 Use the chart to make questions and short answers about how to be a good English speaker.

How to be a good English speaker.	need to/have to	needn't/don't have to
be English		
listen in class		
speak English as much as possible		
live in England		
do your homework		
learn new vocabulary		
spend a lot of money		

1 *Do you need to be English? No, you don't.*
   ....

2 ....

3 ....

4 ....

5 ....

6 ....

7 ....

MARK: ..../6

TOTAL: ..../20

Photocopiable page 22

UNIT 7 TEST

1 Complete the sentences.

1 I ....**had lunch**.......... in a restaurant yesterday.

    had a bath   had a haircut   had lunch

2 I .... at the swimming pool.

    had a business meeting   had dinner

    had a shower

3 I .... with my mum when I

    came home from my drama society yesterday

    evening.

    had breakfast   had a party   had a cup of tea

4 I .... with my teacher about

    my homework.

    had dinner   had a talk   had a drink

MARK: ..../3

2 Match the verbs with their past forms.

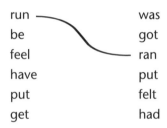

run	was
be	got
feel	ran
have	put
put	felt
get	had

MARK: ..../5

3 Read about Banu's school trip to the zoo. Choose and circle the correct verb form.

My mum normally makes me eat breakfast but today I just *(had)/have* time for a cup of tea. I normally *walk/walked* to school but today I got the bus into town and *meet/met* my teacher and class at the bus station. We all *walk/walked* to the zoo together. The zoo was great. I usually *go/went* to my friend's house after school but today I *come/came* straight home to tell my mum all about it. I don't normally *enjoy/enjoyed* school days but I *enjoyed/enjoy* this one.

MARK: ..../7

4 Complete the questions to go with these answers.

1 .....**What do you have for breakfast?**.....

    I have tea and toast

2 .... breakfast this morning?

    I didn't have any.

3 .... Thursdays?

    I normally go swimming.

4 .... last Thursday?

    I went to my aunt's house and then I went swimming.

5 .... after school?

    I usually do my homework.

6 .... after school yesterday?

    I did my homework and I watched TV.

MARK: ..../5

TOTAL: ..../20

Photocopiable page 23

UNIT 8 TEST

1 Look at this page from a magazine and label the different parts of the page.

~~paragraph~~ heading photo caption column

1 ....

2 ....paragraph........

3 ....

4 ....

5 ....

SPORTS DAY SUCCESS

GIRL BREAKS SCHOOL RECORD

MARK: ..../4

2 Put these sentences into the passive.

1 I send our reporter to get the story.

Our reporter is sent to get the story..........

2 I phone people.

....

3 I correct mistakes.

....

4 I arrange the text in columns on the page.

....

5 I choose photos and illustrations.

....

6 He interviews people from the magazine.

....

7 Tim writes the stories.

....

MARK: ..../6

3 Put these sentences into the active.

1 The story is written by a team of writers.

A team of writers write the story..........

2 The models are made by Carole.

....

3 The scenery is painted by the artists.

....

4 A frame of film is taken by the cameraman.

....

5 The models are moved each time by Carole.

....

6 The sound effects are recorded by Nigel.

....

MARK: ..../5

4 Put *is* or *are* into the following sentences.

1 The photos ...**are**... taken by a team of cameramen.

2 The book .... written by an author.

3 The story .... created by a team of writers.

4 The newspaper .... edited by Peter Robson.

5 The cartoons .... drawn by a group of artists.

6 The newspapers .... sold by newsagents.

MARK: ..../5

TOTAL: ..../20

Photocopiable page 24

UNIT 9 TEST

1 Complete these sentences with *was* or *were*.

1 They ......**were**....... painting the door when the earthquake began.

2 He .... driving home.

3 The children .... playing in the street.

4 Henry and Mary .... walking to the cinema.

5 The police .... searching everywhere.

6 She .... eating her lunch.

MARK: ..../5

2 Join the sentences using when.

1 He was running. The tree fell down.

   He was running when the tree fell down.

2 She was cooking. There was a knock at the door.

   ....

   ....

3 They were cycling. A policeman stopped them.

   ....

   ....

4 She was picking grapes. The volcano erupted.

   ....

   ....

5 She was walking the dog. Her family arrived.

   ....

   ....

6 I was writing a letter. The phone rang.

   ....

   ....

MARK: ..../5

3 Complete the text with *was/were* or *when*.

It was 5 o'clock in the afternoon and people

[1] .... hurrying home from work

[2] .... the storm began.

Peter Goodman said 'I [3] .... coming out of my office [4] .... there was a huge clap of thunder. I saw the building opposite go up in flames. It was struck by lightning'. Buses and taxis [5] .... waiting at the nearby traffic lights [6] .... the building burst into flames.

Glenda Philips was on a bus. 'I [7] .... reading my newspaper [8] .... I saw a huge flame light up the sky. I was terrified. My friend was saying goodbye [9] .... the thunder began. It's a miracle no one was hurt. We [10] .... very lucky.'

MARK: ..../10

TOTAL: ..../20

© Oxford University Press 1998

Photocopiable page 25

UNIT 10 TEST

1 **Match the objects with the materials they are made of.**

1	bottle		wool
2	shoes		cotton
3	Coke can		plastic
4	pencil		glass
5	lunch box		paper
6	jumper		leather
7	cards		aluminium
8	T-shirt		wood

MARK: .... /7

2 **Make sentences using *if* and *will*.**

1 Waste paper/too many trees cut down.

   If you waste paper, too many trees will be cut down.

2 Have showers instead of baths/save water.

   ....
   ....

3 Not recycle glass bottles/waste resources.

   ....
   ....

4 Buy fur coats/animals endangered.

   ....
   ....

5 Throw litter on ground/town dirty.

   ....
   ....

6 Use things again/save money.

   ....
   ....

7 Bicycle instead of car/stop pollution.

   ....
   ....

8 Switch off lights/save electricity.

   ....
   ....

MARKS: ..../7

3 **Make sentences using *should* and *shouldn't*.**

1	drop litter	(✗)
2	plant trees	(✔)
3	save water	(✔)
4	recycle glass	(✔)
5	waste paper	(✗)
6	buy fur coats	(✗)
7	save electricity	(✔)

1 You shouldn't drop litter. ....

2 ....

3 ....

4 ....

5 ....

6 ....

7 ....

MARK: .... /6

TOTAL: .... /20

Photocopiable page 26

UNIT 11 TEST

1 Complete the sentences with adjectives from the box.

> jealous depressed ~~confident~~ moody
> excited worried

1 I have done lots of revision and am ..**confident**.. about my exams.

2 When Georgia showed me her new clothes and told me about her holiday, I felt

....

3 When I was in hospital and couldn't see my friend, I felt ....

4 I am very .... about my exams. I haven't done enough revision.

5 He is so .... One minute he is happy, the next minute he is sad.

6 I've won a holiday in America! I'm so

....

MARK: .... /5

2 Match 1–6 with a–f to make sentences giving advice.

1 You feel tired? If I were you, ..**e**..

2 You're going to France? If I were you, ...

3 You need more money? If I were you, ...

4 You want to feel scared? If I were you, ...

5 You want to go to the party? If I were you, ...

6 You look ill. If I were you, ...

a I'd learn the language.

b I'd see that horror film at the cinema.

c I'd go outdoors more often.

d I'd wait for an invitation.

e I'd go to bed.

f I'd get a job.

MARK: .... /5

3 Make sentences giving advice.

1 I'm always late for school.
   If I were you, I'd get up earlier.

2 I left my homework at home.

   ....

3 I'm always tired.

   ....

4 I'm bored.

   ....

5 I don't get enough pocket money.

   ....

6 I want to do really well in my exams.

   ....

MARK: .... /5

4 Circle the best word to complete the sentences.

1 If you don't like meeting new people, you are
   a shy
   b jealous
   c optimistic

2 If you think the future will be good, you are
   a worried
   b scared
   c optimistic

3 If you do something silly and everyone sees, you feel
   a shy
   b embarrassed
   c jealous

4 If everyone likes you, you are
   a optimistic
   b confident
   c popular

5 If you think the future will be bad, you are
   a confident
   b pessimistic
   c angry

6 If you do not feel confident about yourself, you are
   a tired
   b insecure
   c pessimistic

MARK: .... /5

TOTAL: ..../20

© Oxford University Press 1998

Photocopiable page 27

UNIT 12 TEST

1 Complete these sentences with words from the box.

| could | believe | on | ~~true~~ | can't | up |

1 England won the World Cup? It can't be
   true .
   ....

2 You're 25? Yes, I can .... that.

3 You've bought a house in New York? I think
   you're having me ....

4 He says he went to Spain in the holidays. I
   think he's making it ....

5 They have been to America? Well, it
   .... be true.

6 They have been to the sun? That ....
   be true.

MARK: .... /5

**2 Use the present perfect tense to complete
these sentences.**

1 We are not doing the exercise as we
   have done ...... (do) it already.

2 I .... (eat) Indian food. It's
   delicious.

3 She .... (buy) the most
   beautiful coat I have seen.

4 The band .... (made) a great
   new record.

5 You .... (see) the film already,
   haven't you?

6 English is easier to speak now I ....
   (be) to England.

7 It .... (be) raining for two
   hours.

8 I saw Peter yesterday but I ....
   (see) him today.

9 I .... (eat) so much food today.

MARKS: .... /8

**3 Choose the correct word to complete the
sentences.**

1 I've .... my coat.
   A lost
   B lose
   C find

2 Have you .... to Athens?
   A seen
   B been
   C went

3 We have .... three cups of tea today.
   A drink
   B drank
   C drunk

4 The woman has .... three books already.
   A written
   B write
   C wrote

5 I have .... a tractor on my uncle's farm.
   A drive
   B rode
   C driven

6 The team have never .... a match!
   A won
   B win
   C lose

7 I have never .... to Scotland.
   A gone
   B went
   C been

MARK: .... /7

TOTAL: .... /20

Photocopiable page 28

UNIT 13 TEST

1 Complete these sentences using the words in the box.

crashing	following	drowning
flying	falling	

1 A dream about .... off a mountain would be very frightening.

2 Dreams about .... are very common.

3 I hate water. I really worry about ....

4 He dreamed about .... his father's car.

5 There was something .... me down a long corridor.

MARK: .... /5

2 Complete these sentences with the correct form of the verb in brackets. Use the past simple or present perfect.

1 ..*Have*.... you ever ..*been*.. (be) to Egypt?

2 She .... (have) lots of nightmares recently.

3 I .... (go) to Ankara last year.

4 I .... (eat) Mexican food, but not Chinese food.

5 .... you .... (try) French food?

6 He .... (dream) about flying again last night.

7 .... you ever .... (meet) a famous person?

8 He .... (be) to America many times.

9 She .... (not) .... (do) her homework yet.

10 .... you .... (live) here five years ago?

11 How long .... they .... (know) her?

MARK: .... /10

3 Now turn these questions into statements.

1 Have you dreamed about your football team?
   You have dreamed about your football team.
   ....

2 Has she seen the new Spielberg film?
   ....

3 Did you enjoy seeing the play?
   ....

4 Have we studied theses tenses before?
   ....

5 Has he met her?
   ....

6 Did I meet them last week?
   ....

MARK: ..../5

TOTAL: .... /20

Photocopiable page 29

UNIT 14 TEST

1 Use the words in the box to label the activities.

1 aerobics ....

2 ....

3 ....

4 ....

5 ....

6 ....

7 ....

8 ....

9 ....

swimming   martial arts   snow-boarding
rock-climbing   ~~aerobics~~   yoga
windsurfing   cycling   weight-training

MARK: ..../8

2 Match the colloquial expressions with their equivalents.

super-fit —————— try it
guy ——————— very fit
really into   learn to do it
pick   really keen on
couldn't wait to   frightening
scary   not doing very much
get the hang of it   man
just sitting around   choose
have a go at it   immediately wanted to

MARK: .... /8

3 Look at the pictures of Levent. Are these sentences true or false?

1 He used to be fit.   (True)/ False

2 He used to have long hair.   True / False

3 He didn't use to be poor.   True / False

4 He didn't use to be popular.   True / False

5 He used to be fit.   True / False

MARK: .... /4

TOTAL: .... /20

Photocopiable page 30

UNIT 15 TEST

1 Match the two halves of the sentence.

1 If he drank less coffee,	she wouldn't have to stay up so late.
2 If she took some exercise,	she would be fitter.
3 If she started work earlier,	he would be able to sleep.
4 If he ate a balanced diet,	he would be more organized.
5 If he made a revision timetable,	she wouldn't feel so worried.
6 If she talked to someone,	he would have more energy.

MARK: .... /5

2 Make one second conditional sentence.

1 I'm always late for school. Get up earlier.

   If you got up earlier, you wouldn't be late for school.

2 I forget to do my homework. Write your homework in your homework diary.

   ....
   ....

3 I fail all my exams. Do more revision.

   ....
   ....

4 All my answers in class are wrong. Listen to your teacher.

   ....
   ....

5 I haven't got enough money for lunch. Don't spend so much on sweets.

   ....
   ....

6 I don't have any friends. Be more friendly.

   ....
   ....

MARK: .... /10

3 Make sentences using *should* or *shouldn't*.

1 Do your homework.
   You should do your homework.

2 Don't drink too much coffee.
   ....

3 Make a revision timetable.
   ....

4 Take some exercise.
   ....

5 Eat a balenced diet.
   ....

6 Saty up late.
   ....

MARK: .... /5

TOTAL: ..../20

© Oxford University Press 1998

Key to tests

UNIT 1 TEST

❶

Student's pictures should include the following labels:

  giraffe (next to head)

  elephant (next to ears)

  shark (next to teeth)

  tiger (next to body)

  camel (next to one of legs)

  eagle (next to one of feet)

❷

2	How much	5	Which	8	How many
3	How many	6	How far	9	Where
4	How fast	7	How long		

❸

2	Do … travel	4	Can … hear	6	Is
3	Are there	5	Have … got	7	Does … come

UNIT 2 TEST

❶

2	Put	4	Spread	6	Keep
3	Cut; mix	5	Add		

❷

grain – rice

fruit and vegetables – chillies, potatoes

dairy products – yoghurt, cheese

meat and fish – chicken, beef

other – oil

❸

2	is served	4	is made	6	are made
3	are filled	5	Is … filled	7	are served

UNIT 3 TEST

❶

2 He's going to fall off

3 They're going to dive into

4 He's going to climb up

5 She's going to land on

6 They're going to jump over

❷

2 Are they/the stunts going to be dangerous?

3 Is Kevin going to do all the stunts?

4 When is he going to practise his stunt?

5 How fast is he going to ride?

6 Are they going to film the stunt tomorrow?

UNIT 4 TEST

❶

2	took	6	saw	9	wore
3	went	7	weren't	10	didn't rain
4	perform	8	was	11	began
5	use				

❷

1	lights	3	stage	5	audience
2	scenery	4	seats		

❸

2	caught	4	fell	6	made
3	bought	5	told		

UNIT 5 TEST

❶

2	short	4	unintelligent	6	slim (thin)
3	unattractive	5	unfriendly		

❷

2	look worried.	5	look intelligent.
3	is fat.	6	looks attractive.
4	looks calm.	7	is tall.

❸

2	clearly	4	slowly	6	carefully
3	nervously	5	politely		

❹

2 present simple

3 past simple – irregular verb

4 present continuous

5 *will*

UNIT 6 TEST

❶

1	stamp collecting	5	football
2	aerobics	6	making jewellery
3	chess	7	playing an instrument
4	horse-riding	8	making models

❷

2	need/have to have	5	don't have to be
3	have/need to	6	have/need to
4	needn't/don't have to	7	have/need to

❸

2 Do you have/need to listen in class? Yes, you do.

3 Do you have/need to speak English as much as possible? Yes, you do.

4 Do you have/need to live in England? No, you don't.

5 Do you have/need to do your homework? Yes, you do.

6 Do you have/need to learn new vocabulary? Yes, you do.

7 Do you have/need to spend a lot of money? No, you don't.

UNIT 7 TEST

❶

2 had a shower

3 had a cup of tea

4 had a talk

❷

be	was		put	put
feel	felt		get	got
have	had			

❸

2 walk   5 go   8 enjoyed

3 met   6 came

4 walked   7 enjoy

❹

2 What did you have for breakfast this morning?

3 What do you normally do on Thursdays?

4 What did you do last Thursday?

5 What do you usually you do after school?

6 What did you do after school yesterday?

UNIT 8 TEST

❶

1 heading 3 caption 4 column 5 photo

❷

2 People are phoned.

3 Mistakes are corrected.

4 The text is arranged in columns on the page.

5 Photos and illustrations are chosen.

6 People from the magazine are interviewed.

7 The stories are written by Tim.

❸

2 Carole makes the models.

3 The artists paint the scenery.

4 The cameraman takes a frame of film.

5 Carole moves the models each time.

6 Nigel records the sound effects.

❹

2 is   3 is   4 is   5 are   6 are

UNIT 9 TEST

❶

2 was   3 were   4 were   5 were   6 was

❷

2 She was cooking when there was a knock at the door.

3 They were cycling when a policeman stopped them.

4 She was picking grapes when the volcano erupted.

5 She was walking the dog when her family arrived.

6 I was writing a letter when the phone rang.

❸

1 were   5 were   9 when

2 when   6 when   10 were

3 was   7 was

4 when   8 when

UNIT 10 TEST

❶

shoes – leather   jumper – wool

Coke can – aluminium   cards – paper

pencil – wood   T-shirt – cotton

lunch box – plastic

❷

2 If you have showers instead of baths, you will save water.

3 If you do not recycle glass bottles, you will waste resources.

4 If you buy fur coats, animals will be endangered.

5 If you throw litter on the ground, the town will be dirty.

6 If you use things again, you will save money.

7 If you use a bicycle instead of a car, you will stop pollution.

8 If you switch off lights, you will save electricity.

❸

2 You should plant trees.

3 You should save water.

4 You should recycle glass.

5 You shouldn't waste paper.

6 You shouldn't buy fur coats.

7 You should save electricity.

UNIT 11 TEST

❶

2 jealous   4 worried   6 excited

3 depressed   5 moody

❷

2 a   3 f   4 b   5 d   6 e

❸ Possible answers:

2 If I were you, I'd go home and get it.

3 If I were you, I'd get more sleep.

4 If I were you, I'd find something to do.

5 If I were you, I'd get a job.

6 If I were you, I'd start revising.

❹

2 optimistic   5 pessimistic

3 embarrassed   6 insecure

4 popular

UNIT 12 TEST

❶

2 believe   4 up   6 can't

3 on   5 could

❷

2 have eaten   5 have seen   8 haven't seen

3 has bought   6 have been   9 have eaten

4 have made   7 has been

❸

2 been   4 written   6 won

3 drunk   5 driven   7 been

UNIT 13 TEST

❶

1 falling   3 drowning   5 following

2 flying   4 crashing

❷

2 has had   6 dreamt   10 did live

3 went   7 have met   11 have known

4 have eaten   8 has been

5 have tried   9 hasn't done

❸

2 She has seen the new Spielberg film.

3 You enjoyed seeing the play.

4 We have studied these tenses before.

5 He has met her.

6 I met them last week.

UNIT 14 TEST

❶

2 snow-boarding   5 swimming   8 martial arts

3 cycling   6 rock-climbing   9 yoga

4 weight training   7 windsurfing

❷

guy = man

really into = really keen on

pick = choose

couldn't wait = immediately wanted to

scary = frightening

get the hang of = learn to do it

just sitting around = not doing very much

have a go at = try it

❸

2 true   3 true   4 false   5 true

UNIT 15 TEST

❶

2 If she took some exercise, she would be fitter.

3 If she started work earlier, she wouldn't have to stay up so late.

4 If he ate a balanced diet, he should have more energy.

5 If he made a revision timetable, he would be more organized.

6 If she talked to someone, she wouldn't feel so worried.

❷

2 If you wrote your homework in your homework diary, you wouldn't forget to do your homework /it.

3 If you did more revision, you wouldn't fail all your exams.

4 If you listened to your teacher, your answers in class wouldn't be wrong.

5 If you didn't spend so much on sweets, you would have enough money for lunch.

6 If you were more friendly, you would have more friends.

❸

2 You shouldn't drink too much coffee.

3 You should make a revision timetable.

4 You should take some exercise.

5 You should eat a balanced diet.

6 You shouldn't stay up late.

Test dictations

UNIT 1 TEST, QUESTION 1

- Read the set of instructions once while students listen. Then read each separate instruction twice and pause, giving the students time to draw and write.

  Draw the head and neck of a giraffe. Write the word *giraffe* next to the head.
  Draw the ears of an elephant. Write the word *elephant* next to them.
  Draw the teeth of a shark and write the word *shark* next to them.
  Now draw the body of a tiger and write the word *tiger* next to it.
  Draw the four legs of a camel and write the word *camel* next to one of them.
  Draw the feet of an eagle and write the word *eagle* next to one of them.

UNIT 2 TEST, QUESTION 1

- Give the students a few minutes to read through the incomplete recipe.
- Read the recipe once while students listen. Then read each sentence twice and pause, giving the students time to fill in the verb(s).

  1 Cut some rolls in half.
  2 Put butter on them.
  3 Cut an apple into small pieces and mix the pieces with some cheese.
  4 Spread the mixture on the rolls
  5 Add some mayonnaise.
  6 Keep the sandwiches cold until you are ready to eat them.

Word list

This word list contains all the active and receptive vocabulary in the Student's Book (receptive in italic type). The numbers refer to the unit or project page where the word first appears.

A

aboard	76
accountant	10
accountant	14
achievement	12
action	3
active	9
add	8
advantage	7
adverb	5
advert	14
advice	11
aerobics	6
air	5
airport	5
allowed	76
altogether	4
aluminium	10
aluminium foil	10
amazed	14
amazing	12
amazingly	9
angry	4
animated film	8
anxiety	13
anxious	11
anxious	15
appearance	5
apple pie	81
appropriate	1
armchair	7
article	7
ash	9
ashamed	11
associated with	13
astronaut	12
attention	11
attractive	5
audience	4
audition	14
avoid	10

B

badge	6
balanced diet	15
ballet	4
barrel	3
battery	10
based on	3
believe	4
bird	1

birthday	6
birthday present	6
bite	8
blood	1
blue whale	1
bored	11
bottle up	15
bowl	9
breakfast	5
brush (noun)	6
brush (verb)	7
building	3
bungee-jumping	12
burn	4
butter	2
butterfly	1

C

cafe	81
caffeine	15
calm	15
can (noun)	10
calzone	2
camel	1
caption	7
caption	8
carefully	5
carrot	81
carton	10
cassette	6
cast	4
castle	11
casualty	9
cave	13
CD	6
certain	3
chant	15
charity	7
chase	8
check in	5
cheetah	1
chemical (noun)	10
chess	6
chew	15
chihuahua	1
chilli	2
chips	81
chocolate cake	81
chopsticks	10
chorus	4
clearly	3
cliff	3
close friend	10
cloud	9
clown	13
club	6
coin	6
cold	5
collapse	9
collect	6
colloquial	14
column	8
comedy	76

comic (adjective)	7
competitor	79
compliment	11
conclusion	7
conductor	4
confident	11
constantly	15
container	10
contract (noun)	12
contrast	4
cook	2
copy (noun)	8
copy (verb)	11
coral	13
corn	2
corridor	13
cotton	10
cotton (adjective)	6
couple	2
covered	2
crash (noun)	13
crazy	10
cream	2
creative	8
crocodile	1
cry	4
cucumber	2
curry	2
cut down	15
cycling	6
cycling	14

D

daily	7
dairy products	2
daredevil	3
daydream	13
delicious	2
department	8
depressed	11
desert	81
designer	8
destroy	10
dialogue	12
diamond	5
diet (noun)	14
direct (verb)	8
disadvantage	7
disbelief	12
discussion	7
dish	2
disorganized	15
display (verb)	6
distance	1
distribute	8
dive	8
dolphin	1
doomed	76
dramatic	76
dream (noun & verb)	13
dream image	13
dressing room	7
driver	5

drop in the ocean	5
drown	3
during	3

E

Eagle	1
earthquake	9
eccentric	10
edge	3
edit	8
editor	8
egg	2
elephant	1
embarrassed	11
emotion	5
endangered	10
ending	96
energy	10
enormous	9
entrance	7
environment	10
equivalent	7
erupt	9
eruption	9
event	5
exact	3
exactly	4
excellent	76
excited	11
excitement	4
exciting	14
exercise	6
exercise	15
exhausted	15
experience	12
experiment	12
expert	13
explorer	13

F

fabric paint	6
fact	12
fail	13
faint (verb)	11
fall off	3
famous	7
fan	14
fantastic	1
far	1
fashion model	12
fast	14
fat	14
fearless	10
fee	6
feed (verb)	9
female	4
field	9
fight	79
filled	2
fill in	6
film star	7
film studio	12
fish	2

fisherman	9	heart shaped	5	**L**		neck	5
fit (adjective)	6	heavy	1	lack (noun)	15	need to	6
fit (adjective)	15	height	1	land	1	negative	11
fizzy drink	15	hero	5	Latin America	1	neighbour	10
flame	3	hexagon	79	lava	9	nervous	11
flash (noun)	9	hideaway	13	lay	1	nervously	5
flood	13	high	5	layout	8	net	9
flour	2	hit record	12	lead-up	15	new potatoes	81
fly	1	hobby	6	leather	10	next door	10
fold	8	Home Economics	2	length	1	nightmare	15
folk dancing	6	hopeful	6	letters page	83	noise	3
forbidden	76	horse-riding	6	lettuce	2	normal	7
forest	4	hot	5	lies	83	novel (noun)	5
forgetful	76	hot-air balloon	12	lightning	4	novelist	13
fork	2	how	1	line	8	nowadays	4
form (noun)	6	hurt	79	lip	3		
fresh air	14			liquid (noun)	12	**O**	
friendly	5	**I**		litre	1	obvious	11
frighten	8	ice-skating	6	live	4	octopus	13
frightening	13	ignore	11	long	1	office	7
fruit	17	illustration	8	love story	76	office party	7
fruit salad	81	imaginary	12	luxury	12	omelette	2
fur	10	immediately	5			onion	2
future	3	inactive	9	**M**		open-air	4
		increase	15	magazine	8	optimistic	11
G		Individual players	79	mailbox	14	orbit (verb)	12
galaxy	1	indoors	8	main course	81	orchestra	4
game shows	78	ingredients	2	made with	2	organized	15
garbage	10	inhabitant	9	make sense	9	overworked	11
garbage can	10	insecure	11	make up	4		
gardener	13	inside	2	marry	12	**P**	
garlic	2	instructor	14	Mars	12	pack (verb)	8
general knowledge	1	instrument	6	martial arts	14	packaging	10
Geology	6	in the middle of	5	mash	2	painting	6
get the hang of	14	intelligent	5	mask	4	panic (noun)	15
giraffe	1	intention	3	material	10	paper bag	10
girlfriend	77	interrupt	9	meat	2	paragraph	8
Gladiators	79	interview	7	mend	9	pay a price	10
glass (material)	10	invent	9	menu	81	penfriend	6
god	9	intonation	1	metre	1	perform	4
golden	12	iron (verb)	7	mess	7	performer	4
grain	2	island	5	milk	2	personality	5
grape	9	issue	8	millionaire	12	pessimistic	11
guest	7	ivory	10	miserable	11	phobia	11
guide (noun)	9			mix	2	phone-in	11
guilty	11	**J**		mixing bowl	2	photographer	8
gun	5	jealous	11	mixture	2	physically	14
gunge	7	jetski	3	mnemonic	15	pick	9
guy	14	jewellery	6	model (noun)	6	picture library	8
gym	14	jogging	15	moody	11	picture researcher	8
gymnastics	6	join	6	mosquito	8	pilot	3
		journey	10	motorcycle	3	pizza	81
H		joy	13	mountaineer	12	plan (noun)	9
haircut	11	jug	9	movement	4	plane	3
handkerchief	10	jump out of	3	multi-coloured	15	planned	3
handsome	77			mushroom	2	plastic	7
hang	3	**K**		musical	4	plastic	10
harm (verb)	10	key (verb)	8			platform	14
hard boiled egg	2	key word	12	**N**		playwright	4
have a go	14	kill	9	nail	15	pleasant	13
have to	6	kilogram	1	napkin	10	pleasure	5
heading	8	kilometre	1	nearly	1	plenty of	15
health	10	kiwi	1	necessary	6	plot	77

Oxford University Press,
Great Clarendon Street,
Oxford OX2 6DP

Oxford New York
Auckland Bangkok Buenos Aires Cape Town
Chennai Dar es Salaam Delhi Hong Kong Istanbul Karachi
Kolkata Kuala Lumpur Madrid Melbourne Mexico City Mumbai Nairobi
São Paulo Shanghai Singapore Taipei Tokyo Toronto

and an associated company in Berlin

OXFORD and OXFORD ENGLISH
are trade marks of Oxford University Press

ISBN 0 19 435906 9

© Oxford University Press 1998
First published 1998
Second impression 2002

Illustrations by David Eaton, Margaret Jones and Gary Rees.
Cover illustration by Michael Brownlow.

Typeset by Oxford University Press

Printed in Spain by Unigraf